THE BEST DEVOTIONS OF

# Thelma Wells

WOMEN OF FAITH™

# THE BEST DEVOTIONS OF

# Thelma Wells

**ZONDERVAN™**

GRAND RAPIDS, MICHIGAN 49530

ZONDERVAN™

*The Best Devotions of Thelma Wells*
Copyright © 2001 by Thelma Wells

Requests for information should be addressed to:
Zondervan, *Grand Rapids, Michigan 49530*

**Library of Congress Cataloging-in-Publication Data**

Wells, Thelma.
    The best devotions of Thelma Wells/Thelma Wells.
       p. cm.
    ISBN 0-310-24173-1 (pbk.)
    1. Christian women—Prayer-books and devotions—English.
    I. Title.
    BV4844 .W45 2001
    242—dc21                          2001026972

Published in association with the literary agency of Alive Communications, Inc., 7680 Goddard Street, Suite 200, Colorado Springs, CO 80920.

*Interior design by Beth Shagene*

*Printed in the United States of America*

01 02 03 04 05 06 07 08 /❖ DC/ 10 9 8 7 6 5 4 3 2 1

*Bazillions of people have influenced my life.*
*Many of these people are contributors*
*to the works in this book, including my family*
*and over one million women who have attended*
*the Women of Faith Conferences.*
*Thank you ladies for your loyalty and support.*

*These devotionals are dedicated to you*
*for your inspiration and empowerment.*
*As you read the words on these pages remember*
*that, "In Christ, you can BEE your best!"*

# Contents

# Foreword by Patsy Clairmont

If I could freeze-frame shots of Thelma Well's life for you, I'd make sure you saw what I've witnessed over the past five years. When you work and travel with someone that long, you have the opportunity to see a person from many camera angles. And I assure you, every frame has enriched my life.

For an individual who has suffered as much prejudice as Thelma has, I'm amazed at her heart's expansiveness for all people. Maybe the treatment she has received is why she is so tenderhearted and inclusive—she knows what it feels like to be ignored and deliberately abused. Drawing on Christ's example, Thelma embraces the downtrodden, the hurting, and the sick. I've watched her gather ailing women into her arms and utter prayers of faith over them. I've watched as she has wiped their tears and directed them into God's Word. And I've seen countless women walk away heartened.

A mantle of praise rests on Thelma's life, and I'd want to capture that for you to see. You hear it in her soul-searching music, and you experience it in her melodic attitudes. Praise permeates her counsel as she reminds us, "When praises go up, blessings come down."

Thelma's appreciation button is always set on high. She's not given to griping or taking what's bestowed on her for granted. I believe her high level of gratitude has caused the rest of us on the Women of Faith staff to raise our own bars. But she displays more than a positive atti-tude; she exudes a "God is good" way of thinking that goes to the marrow of her bones.

Often Thelma's family members have joined us at conferences where I've enjoyed watching their deep respect and love for her. From sons-in-law to grand-daughters to daughters to her beloved husband, George, they watch her with pride. And I understand why. Her walk and her talk line up with her Spirit-filled messages. No wonder her family is so drawn to Jesus.

During the 2001 conferences, Thelma's daughters danced before the Lord prior to Thelma's speaking. They chose "Jesus Loves Me," sung by their mom. These beau-tiful young women moved with grace and joy, pleasing the attendees and delighting their momma. Big tears of gratitude filled Thelma's eyes, as she recognized afresh the blessing of having children who love the Lord too.

I'd also want to freeze-frame for you the twinkle in Thelma's eye; that immediately alerts you to her fun-lov-ing ways. Her laugh starts at her festively clad feet (the woman loves shoes) and makes its way right up to her shoulder, which is adorned with a bumblebee pin (she never leaves home without one). In the years I've known this sweet lady, I've never heard her laugh at others' expense. But I have, on a number of occasions, heard her chortle over her own faux pas. She takes God seriously and herself lightly.

One of my favorite images of Thelma is her pouring over Scripture in search of truth. Her Bible's worn pages testify to her constant pursuit of holiness and her own personal desire for God's counsel. Her prayers are filled with his principles and her songs extol his virtues. From her passion for Psalm 23 to the Lord's Prayer, Thelma is an alpha and omega lady. From "in the beginning" in

Genesis to the amen of Revelation, she dines on his Word and reminds us also to "taste and see that the Lord is good."

And I'd want you to see the new dimension that's been added to my cohort's life since her travels with World Vision to Africa and to India. It seems from my camera angle that God just keeps enlarging her heart's territory. I've noted an even deeper appreciation and sweeter dedication from Thelma to be a woman of faith throughout the world.

So know that when you read *The Best Devotions of Thelma Wells*, you're on solid ground. You will laugh and learn with one who has walked the dusty trail of life and has come through praising. My dear sister will cause you to lift your eyes and your heart to the One who understands you best and loves you most.

## Saying the Three Words

But the greatest of these is love.
1 CORINTHIANS 13:13

For the first eighteen years of my married life, I wanted my husband to say three specific words. Maybe he had said them once or twice but, apparently, so seldom I couldn't recall hearing them.

I would say, "Please, baby, just tell me you love me. Even if you're lying, just say it!"

He would respond, "Why do I have to say *that?* You know I do. It don't make sense to have to say *that* when I show you all the time."

Then I'd beg, "I know you show me, and I appreciate that. But just say it. It won't hurt."

Do I have to tell you that nothing ever came of those conversations?

Now, my husband's background is different from mine. His father had thirty-one sisters and brothers. That's what I said, thirty-one. I have the names and birthdays all recorded to prove it.

They grew up on a huge farm in south Texas where they raised everything they ate. They had cattle, pigs, chickens, sugarcane, vegetables, wheat (and their own flour mill), cotton, fishing tank, and—God forbid—homemade whiskey. The kids worked all the time when they weren't in school. The family lived in a seven-room home in which the bedrooms were nearly as large as some houses. The boys slept in two rooms, and the girls slept in two rooms.

I suppose they were together so much that the words "I love you" never occurred to them to say. At least, not to the boys. They were taught to be men, and men didn't show emotion. Men didn't cry. Men didn't say mushy stuff. That's the environment my husband was raised in.

Me, I'm a city slicker from Dallas. No horses, cows, and pigs for me. The closest I came to a farm was Granny's yard where she planted a patch of greens and beans. Concord grapes grew on the fence, and one year a couple of watermelons showed up in the garden. Three of us lived in our house. We had one bedroom, a sleep sofa, and a rollaway bed on the screened-in front porch. But something was practiced in our house that I will forever appreciate. We often used the words "I love you."

So when I married George, we wrangled over those words and getting him to say them. Years later we hosted our eighteen-year-old daughter's debutante reception. During her presentation she had great things to say about her parents. But one story she told captured the hearts of the two hundred people attending.

"Ever since I was a little girl," Vikki started out, "my mama would tell us she loves us. My father would never tell us. I would say, 'Daddy, I love you,' and he would always say, 'I know it, Vikki.'

"Well, Daddy, I finally figured out what you mean when you say, 'I know it, Vikki.' You're really saying, 'I love you too.' So Daddy, it's all right. Keep on saying what you say, and I'll know what you mean."

That story set everyone off. Some people were sniffing and crying. Some had wet eyes that they tried to dab when no one was looking. Even my macho husband was crying. Mr. Non-Emotional, Won't-Speak-in-Public-Before-a-Large-Group meandered to the microphone and said, "Come here, Vikki, Daddy wants to tell you something." Holding the microphone in one hand and putting his arm around Vikki, he said, "Daddy loves you, Vikki. Daddy's proud of you."

Almost every week since that monumental day in 1981 he's been telling us he loves us. Hallelujah!

Do you enjoy hearing those tender words from your spouse, children, family, and friends? Of course you do. However, to know that we are loved by an omnipotent, omnipresent, omniscient Lord is the grandest feeling of acceptance anyone can have. When other people fail to express their love to us, we can always depend on Jesus.

Imagine Jesus himself saying to you, "Child of mine, I love you with an everlasting love. I love you with unconditional love. I love you because I want to! I love you when others think you are unlovable. I love you when you have sinned and come short of my glory. I love you in the good times and in the bad."

*God, we can't comprehend the depth of your love. We do know that without your loving protection we would be in danger. Without your loving provision we would be in want. Without your loving correction we would remain rebellious. Without your loving care we wouldn't know compassion. Without your loving Son we wouldn't be saved. When we begin to attach strings to our love for someone, even by demanding they tell us they love us, remind us that you have no strings attached to your love. Amen.*

# *The Road to Glory Ain't Always Easy*

In this world you will have trouble. But take heart!
I have overcome the world.
JOHN 16:33

One of the most glorious experiences I've ever had is when I traveled to the Holy Land. A pastor asked me to be the soloist on a trip he was organizing, and after I gladly accepted, twenty-three of my family members and friends joined the entourage.

Everywhere we went brought Bible stories to life, but a couple of Holy Land experiences especially stood out for me. The first was watching my daughter Vikki climb the mountain at Masada. It was a frightening moment for her and me. Vikki, with her free spirit, discovered that once you start to climb a mountain, it's so steep and rough your only option is to keep your sights on finishing and your mind on the rocks and boulders up ahead. You have to keep looking forward and not back, and you have to pray every step of the way that you will make it.

It took Vikki so long to reach the top where the group was waiting for her that I was worried. Others who had started up the mountain with her had arrived looking wild-eyed and fatigued, saying that was not a wise choice. They wished they had ridden the cable cars as most of us had.

When I asked if they had seen Vikki, they said she was having difficulty climbing the mountain, but all of them were in distress and nobody could help anyone else. You can imagine how that made me feel.

Vikki finally arrived at the top. Many of our group were cheering and thanking God that she had survived the ordeal. Vikki's first words were, "Mama, don't ever let me do something like that again. I thought I was going to die!"

That experience taught her the road to glory is difficult with its rocks and boulders, its strain and struggle. But if you keep on keeping on, you can make it. Things aren't always as easy as we would like. Surprises and pitfalls wait for us along the road of life. We're going to sweat and sway, we're going to wonder why things are the way they are, and we're even going to blame other people.

But every road has an end; every mountain has its peak. If we can just hold on and keep climbing, knowing that God is aware of how we're straining, he will bring us up and over the mountains. It's consoling to know God is in control of every part of our journey to glory, even over the steep mountains.

The second experience that especially touched my soul was walking down the Via Dolorosa (The Way of Sorrows) where Jesus painfully walked, carrying his cross and passing by Simon the Cyrene, the man who helped Jesus bear the cross up Golgotha.

But this moving experience turned into a nightmare for one of the pastors traveling with us. He had been to the Holy Land more than twenty-five times and had warned us about pickpockets in the Via Dolorosa crowd and how skillfully they committed their crime. He told us to keep our money on our bodies rather than in purses or satchels. The men should keep their wallets out of their back pockets. He cautioned us to take off any precious jewelry and dress down to keep from being pegged as "rich" tourists. All of us obeyed.

Once a person's belongings were gone, the pastor warned, it would be extremely difficult to catch who did it because the thieves would mingle in the crowd.

The man who had given us these explicit instructions was our only casualty. He had his hand in his pocket holding his money clip inside his passport when a skillful pickpocket whisked his hand into that pocket, taking the passport and the money. The preacher saw nothing. He felt the heist, but it was too late.

The victim preacher told us he had become too sure of himself. He thought he had traveled enough and knew how to keep himself safe.

Doesn't the same thing happen in life? God warns us of danger. We listen and are careful. But then we slough off. Even when we see warning signs, we think we're smart enough and have our act together. We don't listen or pay attention. That's when we fall and fail.

So whether you're climbing mountains or think you have a firm grip on everything that's important to you, you would be wise to look to the Lord. Remain humble and aware that your footing could slip at any time — or you could feel those things that are so precious to you slip from your fingers without warning. We're on the way to glory land, but we ain't there yet!

*Lord, thank you that you give us the endurance to climb every mountain in our path to glory. Help us to keep our eyes fixed on you through it all. And thank you that even when the going gets tough you give us sweet contentment in our souls. Enable us to keep our ears attuned to your warnings for us and not to become cocky or complacent when we think we know the way ahead. Thank you for the protection you extend to us when we listen. Amen.*

*Fire!*

I've heard people say, "If you want anything done right, you have to do it yourself."

I used to say that too, until I realized I didn't have a life because I had so many fires to put out, and someone always seemed to be pouring on more fuel. The stress was overwhelming. My smoke screen of rationalizations for why I needed to be the one to do all those tasks was fast disappearing. I needed help.

Like putting out any fire that's out of hand, I couldn't do this alone. I enlisted the help of others by pledging to myself I would teach appropriate people everything I knew about what I was doing. Projects that used to be mine became ours. Clients I thought only I could handle were delegated to staff. Records I had to have my hands on at all times became the responsibility of others.

Now everyone knows how the system works and is able to keep it going despite a hectic work schedule, deadlines, and putting out those fires. Come to think of it, we don't have many fires to put out because the system works so well. What a relief to know I can travel, take vacations, write books—things that take me away from the office for weeks at a time—and still have a well-run business.

I'm not the first to experience the suffocating effects of thinking I have to do it all to get it right. Nor am I the first to think about delegating as a way to pour water on the fire. Moses' father-in-law, Jethro, saw that he was stressed to the max because he was judging, managing, controlling, budgeting, pastoring, teaching, preaching, and being everything to everybody on the journey from Egypt to the Promised Land. So he told Moses that he needed to delegate a big chunk of his responsibilities. He was a behind-the-scenes fire chief, quietly seeing to it that all the appropriate fire trucks and firefighters were dispatched to bring Moses some relief.

Maybe you have said you need help with all the fires raging in your life: projects at home, work, and church; responsibilities with your friends, family, and coworkers; a calendar filled to bursting. You might have said you would rather do it yourself to make sure it's done right. But one of the most rewarding ways to relate to others is to give them ownership over what's going on. At home the entire family should share in keeping things up around the house. At work people want to be a part of things and to have responsibility with accountability. And others in your life are waiting for you to take some items off your calendar so you have time to spend with them.

First, you have to decide you're tired of fighting these blazes yourself. Then you need to decide who can help and how. Form a bucket brigade and get everyone to pitch in.

Now, one caveat is important to recognize. You have to remember that delegation has few short-term benefits but amazing long-term ones. You see, it takes awhile to complete the delegation process. Training, explaining, and overseeing are all part of it. However, when everyone has tasks and can do them with little supervision, you begin to reap the results and feel relief.

I bet that you have some people to whom you can delegate housework, office work, and church work. Wouldn't it be great not to have the frightening words, "Fire! Another fire!" reverberating in your mind?

*Oh, Lord, when you gave Moses the pattern for delegation and proved over the centuries it can work, it stands to reason that I should follow that pattern when appropriate. Praise you, Lord, that you provide ways for us to be more productive and less stressed. Help me to trust people enough to give them important tasks. Help those to whom I delegate accept the responsibility with confidence and commitment to do a superior job. Amen.*

## *Listen to Your Heart*

My sheep listen to my voice; I know them,
and they follow me.

JOHN 10:27

Do you ever wish you had followed your heart instead of your mind? I do! I wish I had stayed in San Antonio the day after we had finished a Women of Faith conference. We speakers were meeting to discuss plans for 1998, but I had a previous commitment in Lincoln, Nebraska, so I couldn't stay.

Fortunately, I was able to attend the first hour. When Pat, my assistant, came to let me know our ride to the airport was waiting, I thought, *I ought to stay here. I'm not going to Lincoln. I should wait a few minutes.* But then I thought, *Are you crazy? You promised your client in Lincoln you would be there. Suppose you miss the flight? You have to speak at the opening session Monday morning. Git outta here!*

I followed Pat to the waiting car and mentioned to her I thought I should stay. I telephoned my office for messages from the car on the way to the airport. There were none. When I reached the San Antonio airport, I called again. Nothing. In my heart, I still believed I wasn't going to Lincoln.

When I got to my house in Dallas, I turned on the weather channel. What was the first thing I heard? "All power lines are down in Lincoln, Nebraska. This is the worst snowstorm they have had in many years. Travelers' advisories are out all over the state. Airports are closed ..."

I called my client's home in Lincoln. No answer. I called the hotel where the meeting was scheduled and was informed the meeting had been canceled. I called my office and heard a message that sounded frantic. "Thelma, Thelma, if you have not boarded the plane coming to Lincoln, please, please don't. The program has been canceled. We'll call you when the weather is better to let you know if we rescheduled. I sure hope you get this message." There was a second message, "Thelma, do not come to Lincoln today. Will call you later." Still another message, "Thelma, I am to pick you up at the airport. We have not been able to speak with you personally. I will be there, but I hope you won't."

I unpacked my bags, settled down, and told my husband how I wished I had listened to my heart. If I had stayed at the Women of Faith meeting a little longer and called my office a little later, I could have stayed for the entire meeting. In my heart, I sensed what God wanted me to do, but I was too fearful to respond.

You might ask, "Thelma, how do you know it was God directing you? It could have been you talking to yourself because you wanted to be in the meeting!"

Good question! My experience with the prompting of the Holy Spirit has been that when he does, there is an indescribable peace in your body, mind, and spirit that you feel but can't explain to anyone who hasn't experienced it. And, of course, God's Spirit would never direct us to do anything contrary to Scripture, so we have a guidebook that can help us. You've probably said in certain situations, "I knew in my heart that such and such was . . ." Or, "I had a feeling that . . ." Those are probably times God's Spirit is prompting you.

Even though I didn't go to Lincoln that day, I realized more fully that I need to be responsive to the Holy Spirit. I have found him to be the greatest organizer, time manager, administrator, arbitrator, and scheduler.

What will you do when you think you're being prompted by the Holy Spirit to take a certain action? I'd suggest you ask for clarity. Wait for the answer. I can't tell you how you will know when the answer comes, but I can tell you that you will experience peace in your mind, body, and soul that you can't describe. Listen to your heart.

*Divine Master, help us understand when we hear your voice deep within us. When you speak, remind us that, as your children, we know your voice. Help us to trust your instructions and not to be afraid. Amen.*

## *First Impressions*

Do not judge, or you too will be judged.
MATTHEW 7:1

Perhaps you've heard the expression, "You never have a second chance to make a first impression." It's true; the first impression is usually the lasting impression. But, thanks be to God, sometimes we get another chance.

When I first met our friends James and Juanita Tennard, the scene was not pretty. It was about one in the morning. I was expecting our second child. I was fuming angry with my husband because he was out much later than usual. Because I was afraid something had happened to him, I was frustrated and angry.

When I saw the car come up the driveway, I met George at the door—and I didn't greet him with tender, loving care. I stormed at him, "Where have you been? What do you mean coming in here this time of night!"

He tried to explain. "I met my friends from Houston. We went out for dinner. They're in the car waiting to come in to spend the night. I told them you wouldn't mind."

Oh. Immediately, I turned my attention from fussing at him to inviting them into our home. Juanita says I said, "Come on in. Y'all are welcome. I'm not mad at you. I'm fussing at George." She said she was afraid to come in.

But once they got inside the house and I prepared a comfortable bed for them and shared with them my concern for George and why I was upset, they both understood. That fall night in 1963, even though I didn't make a very good first impression, an unwavering friendship began that has lasted over three decades through trials and hardships, good times and bad.

We are together several times during the year including Easter, weddings, anniversaries, graduations, births, and funerals. Their baby daughter, Tammy, started to walk in our living room.

James and Juanita's first impression of me was a mean, angry wife. Even though they remember that incident, they eventually got to know the real Thelma, and they gave me a second chance to create a more favorable impression.

I can't say I did the same during an incident that occurred in the mid-eighties. I walked into a Dallas bank to meet with an executive vice president about customer service training. I went up to the secretary's desk, smiled, and announced my name and my reason for being there. The secretary stopped working, looked me up and down, gave me no response, stood up, and walked off, leaving me standing there. I was appalled. I assumed she had judged me and decided I wasn't worth a nod, grunt, or smirk, let alone a smile or a handshake.

Looking for a friendly face, I found another worker and asked her to let the gentleman know I was there. When I settled into a chair in the vice president's office, I started to tell him of the incident.

He cut me off and said, "What has she done this time?"

"This time! This time! Why is she here?" I asked.

The vice president explained that he often received complaints about her snippy behavior toward customers and coworkers, but he was hoping my seminar would help her to change. I didn't tell him I was no miracle worker, but that's what I was thinking. And even if I had been, I wouldn't want to ply my trade with her. I had no enthusiasm for Ms. Nose-in-the-Air's being in my class. My impression of that woman was set.

Well, surprise. When I taught the customer service class, she was a top participant. She was amiable, kind in her comments, pleasant, positive, polite, and poised. But none of that held any meaning for me. All I could remember was how ugly she had been toward me. I didn't know what caused her turn around. Maybe she had been experiencing a lot of pain in her life. Maybe I didn't have the full story. I didn't care. Nope, her lasting impression remained my first impression of her.

Now, I wasn't following Christ's admonition to give people room to make a second impression. I needed to give her a second chance. After all, that graciousness had been extended to me by James and Juanita—and Christ. That doesn't mean I would have changed my mind, but an entrenched attitude wasn't the way to approach the situation either.

Perhaps you have judged people without giving them a chance to show you who they really are. Maybe you have written a person off as someone you want nothing to do with. Maybe you have decided you can't work with someone on your team. Or maybe you refuse to work with a particular person on a committee at church. You may have even turned that person away from your home. That person just might deserve a second chance to make a first impression.

And how about you? How many times have you conveyed an impression to others you aren't proud of? How often do you wonder why you did or said something that caused another person to get the wrong impression? How often do you appear to be something you aren't?

When I create a wrong first impression, I'm consoled to realize God knows us inside out and outside in. He never has to wonder who we are or what we're up to. And if we behave badly sometimes, he understands what motivates us and accepts us even in our worst moments. I want to be able to do the same for others.

*Dear Lord, sometimes we act and perform in ways that send mixed messages about who we are. We've all made negative first impressions. Help us to be mindful of how we are to create, first and foremost, the impression of Christ's grace and mercy alive in us. Amen.*

# I Like Smart Women

When the queen of Sheba heard about the fame of
Solomon and his relation to the name of the LORD,
she came to test him with hard questions.

1 KINGS 10:1

One of my husband's favorite sayings comes from the
television commercial in which a little child says, "I
like smart women." When I say something he thinks is
helpful, find something he has lost, or make a decision
he thinks shows insight, he says, "I like smart women!"

A number of smart women show their stuff in the
Bible. One of them is the powerful, beautiful queen of
Sheba. Her wit, determination, leadership, negotiation
skills, and willingness to learn about God fascinate me.
Now, isn't that a list we'd all like to have appear behind
our name in the Roster of Life?

The Arabian queen journeyed 1,400 miles to Jerusalem
(we're probably talking camel here; for sure not a jet) to
establish rapport with and learn from the wisest man who
ever lived, King Solomon. I can just see them sitting down
for dinner. She pulls out her pencil, licks its tip, and then
flips open her steno pad filled with the questions she had
thought up on that long journey. Her goal is to see what it
would take to stymie this wise guy.

I can imagine her furiously penning Solomon's words
and forgetting all about the Duck L'Orange on her plate.

For he answered every question on her quiz to her satis-faction. (Why do I think she was a woman who didn't suf-fer fools?)

After the Q & A session, they moved on to a tour of his home. By the time Sheba had admired his well-appointed palace, checked the end tables for dust and found none, noted that the waiters were elegantly dressed and hospitable while the cupbearers were solici-tous, well, she was smitten.

Now, the queen was a woman of great possessions and influence herself, and she had multiple layers of reasons for the diplomatic visit to this king. She wanted to make a deal with Solomon, whose country lay between her land and the sea. She had in mind negotiating an inter-national trade agreement. So she had packed in her lug-gage enticing gifts—gold, spices, and precious stones. Smart woman.

Ms. Sheba went back to Arabia with more than a trade agreement and a steno pad full of information. Her heart was touched by what she had learned of Solomon's God, and she returned to her realm to revolutionize the pagan religions. She introduced the idea of worshiping the true and living God to her people.

When I think about the Queen of Sheba and what she did for the world, I'm convinced that, as fulfilling as hav-ing power, influence, possessions, education, commit-ment, and determination are, the most precious attribute in our lives is seeking and applying godly wisdom.

According to Proverbs, "The fear of the LORD is the beginning of wisdom" (Prov. 9:10). Sheba feared (held in reverence) Solomon's God. As a matter of fact, she earned a commendation from Jesus himself when he said, "The Queen of the South will rise at the judgment with this generation and condemn it; for she came from the ends of the earth to listen to Solomon's wisdom, and now one greater than Solomon is here" (Matt. 12:42).

Have you discovered that the wiser we are the more successful we are in our endeavors? Our business thrives. Our personal and family relationships are intact. Our finances are under control. Our negotiations are fair. Our intellect is improved. Our spiritual lives are enhanced. Our Christian walk is easier.

I thank the Lord for the example of this smart woman who used her intelligence and spiritual openness to show the world that wisdom is the greatest attribute to seek.

*Father, sometimes we can think we're smart women until we find ourselves acting out of our own will without consulting you. When will we learn that wisdom only comes from you? Help us to lean on you as we conduct all of our affairs. Amen.*

# Ah, Sweet Repose

Cast all your anxiety on him because he cares for you.
1 PETER 5:7

Sometimes, despite our best intentions, we find ourselves wandering in a wilderness of anxiety, lost and unable to find our way out. I know. For years I felt that way. Nothing seemed to work; I felt stripped and anxious, unable to determine what my mission in life should be. What was I aiming for? Where was a map out of this hazy land in which I wandered?

It wasn't that I hadn't set goals. It's that I didn't know how to set my sights on God and let him lead me where to go. So, even when I was accomplishing what I had set out to do, I still felt lost.

Until one year when not only was I lost but I also lost everything. My business was at an all-time low, my husband had closed his business, and we had a small heap of money and a big mound of bills. Then I heard Dr. Charles Stanley of In Touch Ministries teach on anxiety. He said that the only way to get rid of anxiety was to humble yourself before the Lord and cast your cares on him.

For four days I thought about what he had said, wondering if it was that simple. By the fourth day, I was broken. I lay sobbing facedown on the floor in my bedroom. I remember praying, "Lord, I give my body, mind, soul, career, and family to you. I give you everything. Teach me your will. And I am determined not to get up from here until I feel some relief."

Much later, I woke up and discovered I was still on the floor. I had been in a deep, restful sleep. It must have been what the Bible calls "sweet sleep" because I awakened singing. I hadn't had a song in my heart for months. That was a turning point for me.

So it was no surprise what transpired a couple of years later while I was in a gathering with twenty-five well-established businesswomen. As we sat around chatting, drinking tea, and eating finger foods, one of them said, "Let's share our goals for next year." (The meeting was held toward the end of the year.) Each woman unfurled her major goal for the group:

"I'm going to expand my business into new areas."

"I will gross a half million next year."

"I want to add two new staff members."

"I just added a new administrator; now I can concentrate on starting another business."

"I plan to write my first book."

"I hope to take more time for my family."

"I'm going back to school."

Everyone had a goal. Finally, it was my turn. "I don't have any goals." The group looked puzzled. I'm sure most of them were thinking, *No goals? How can she be successful without goals?*

I continued, "I used to set goals all the time, but I've decided that wherever God leads me, I'll follow."

The room was quiet. I had been the last to speak. I'm sure a few ladies thought I was being irresponsible. But I didn't care. I had traveled through the wilderness of anxiety to come to this conclusion. Now, it's true that goals help us to be disciplined and to aim our energies toward accomplishing what we've set out to do. So goals in and of themselves aren't bad. But for me, setting goals and not leaning on God had led me into a perplexing and fretful place I didn't want to go back to. I had learned that first I needed to humbly go before God and give him my concerns. Then he will provide me with direction. But the relinquishment and sweet repose were what I wanted to concentrate on since that day on the floor.

You may be in the same wilderness I was, anxiously wandering around, feeling aimless, and without a map, fearful disaster is headed toward you. Relinquish your anxieties to God. For he cares for you. Directions will come in God's good time — and so will sweet sleep.

*Lord, teach me to come humbly before you, giving you all my concerns that weigh so much to me but are so light to you. I need you to lighten my load. Thank you for your gentle care for me. Amen.*

## Snoozin'

Do not be afraid or discouraged, for the LORD God, my God,
is with you. He will not fail you or forsake you.
1 CHRONICLES 28:20

I don't know whether I'm getting old and forgetful or I'm just losing it. But I have evidence it's possible both are true. Two times recently I've missed events my heart was set on attending.

A couple of beautiful, intelligent young ladies who grew up in the church I attend set their educational goals and attained them. I was invited to the much deserved graduation and the everybody-will-be-there, after-graduation celebration. I was set to go!

On that particular Saturday I ran the usual errands and laid out my clothes for the graduation. Then I decided to take a fifteen-minute nap. I have a reputation around my house for being one of the world's fastest sleepers. Fifteen minutes of sleep rejuvenates me. So, I settled down for a quick nap. That little nap turned into eight hours of sleep.

I couldn't believe it. Obviously, I had missed the graduation and the celebration. I was heartsick! How could I explain to Geri, Ruby, and Earl that I slept through it all?

Now I better understand how Peter, James, and John felt when Jesus asked them to watch with him just one hour and those guys were caught napping. Their hearts probably dropped to the bottom of their stomachs too. Not to mention their pulse rate increasing and their eyes becoming wide and watery. Their embarrassment was probably as visible as the wrinkles in their slept-in clothes.

Like me, the disciples probably started making a mental list of the ways they could have avoided missing one of the most important times in their friend's life. I thought that my story would have ended differently if I had sat in the chair and nodded; if I had fought the sleep and simply stayed awake; if I had asked someone to wake me up at a certain time.

All those ifs were too late. The damage was done. I had disappointed my friends and myself.

Then, I couldn't believe it, something similar happened during the Christmas holidays. Christi at New Life Clinics asked me to be the surprise guest for the employees at their annual Christmas dinner. I agreed. But I didn't write it down.

The day of the event, I was packing my office to move to another location. I kept feeling this annoying tug that said, "You're supposed to do something today." But I couldn't for all the moving boxes in Dallas think of what it was.

On Christmas Day someone asked me how the surprise appearance at New Life had gone. Oh, no! I felt "gone," all right. My heart was sick. As a matter of fact, every time I think of it even now, my stomach quivers, my heart beats faster, my head feels strained, and my body feels drained. I still want to kick myself.

Have you ever been in a similar situation? Did you face up to it (red-faced and all) and accept responsibility? Or did you avoid the issue and pretend it didn't happen?

Each time I forced myself to face up to what I had done. Telling the truth cleared my conscience and showed honesty. Everyone I had failed seemed to understand.

Wouldn't it be horrible if Jesus slept through some events in our lives? We would call him, but he couldn't hear the call because he was trying to rest. Wouldn't it be frightening to think he could forget our requests? Wouldn't it be tragic if he were so busy he couldn't remember what we talked to him about?

Thank God we don't have to endure that kind of treatment from our Lord! Psalm 121:4 says, "Indeed, he who watches over Israel will neither slumber nor sleep." It's consoling to know God not only doesn't sleep, but also he doesn't even get drowsy. We can depend on him to attend to our every need twenty-four hours a day, seven days a week. That gives us peace.

Isaiah 49:15 asks a poignant question about forgetfulness. "Can a mother forget the baby at her breast and have no compassion on the child she has borne? Though she may forget, I will not forget you!" Hallelujah, we are never forgotten! Even when our very own mother might not remember us, God can be depended on.

It's a bitter pill to think that we let others down. We disappoint loved ones. We inconvenience people we care about. But how wonderful, how beautiful, how comforting to know we have a God who is always near to console and cheer, just when we need him most.

*God of grace, thank you that we can depend on you to be available every minute of every day. Thank you that there are some things you can't do, like doze off or forget. Thank you that when we unintentionally disappoint our friends and loved ones, you give them a spirit of forgiveness. Amen.*

# Daddy Harrell and the Prayer Meetin'

Who wants all men to be saved and to come
to a knowledge of the truth.
1 TIMOTHY 2:4

In God's infinite plan for my life, he allowed me to be born out of wedlock to a crippled girl whose parents were so embarrassed by the situation they forced her to leave their home and find her own way. When I was about two years old, my mother and I both became very ill. Granny, my great-grandmother, convinced my mother to let me live at Granny's house so she could nurse me back to health. During my convalescence, Granny and my great-grandfather, Daddy Harrell, became very attached to me. So, when my mother got well, the decision was made to allow me to stay with my great-grandparents. Granny always told me that my mother didn't give me away, she just let them keep me while she worked and tried to make it on her own.

Daddy Harrell and I became best friends. He was blind, but as soon as I was old enough to learn my way around the neighborhood, I became his eyes. I held his hand and led him down the street to Taplett's Fish Market, to the doctor's office, to visit his friends, or to church.

One of our favorite after-school games was "prayer meeting." The little parlor of our garage apartment became the St. John Missionary Baptist Church. The old sofa was the pew, and a tall-backed chair was the pulpit. Together, Daddy Harrell and I sang the old, metered hymns of the church and hollered out long-winded prayers, the kind late-arriving church attendees hated because it would be so long before the praying ended and they were allowed to be seated.

I remember some of them saying, "Honey, you better get inside the church before Daddy Harrell starts praying. You know he don't know how to stop once he gets wound up."

Daddy Harrell sang with more enthusiasm than talent, but he could remember every word of his two favorite hymns, "When the Battle Is Over We Shall Wear a Crown" and "I Shall Not Be Moved." His slightly off-key baritone wavered alongside my loud, childish voice. Together we belted out songs and prayed down fire and brimstone in our make-believe church.

When I think of Daddy Harrell, I feel love all over. His tolerance, patience, and most importantly, his presence was like that of God. I know my heavenly Father because I have seen him in the people I love.

God knew my great-grandparents' nurturing would be the catalyst that would propel me to learn the truths about who God is and how he works in our everyday lives. And those play prayer meetings would be so engraved in my heart I would transfer praying into a life-long activity and into the lives of my children and grandchildren.

Through the examples of my Granny and Daddy Harrell, I would internalize the power of the names of God. In my prayer time I can call him:

Jehovah Yahweh (I Am Who I Am)
Jehovah Jireh (The Lord Will Provide)
Jehovah Nissi (The Lord Is My Banner)
Jehovah Shalom (The Lord Is Peace)
Jehovah Shammah (The Lord Is There)
Jehovah Tsebaoth (The Lord of Hosts)
Jehovah Elohe Israie (The Lord God of Israel)
Jehovah Rapha (The Lord God Has Healed)

Just as Daddy Harrell trusted me to lead him from place to place without fear of falling or being run over by a car, he taught me to trust God by turning over to him my fears and anxieties. Daddy Harrell's eyesight prevented him from reading, but he had memorized some Scripture while he still had sight. His remedy for my fear was Psalm 23:4, "Even though I walk through the valley of the shadow of death, I will fear no evil, for you are with me; your rod and your staff, they comfort me." He recited that verse to me often.

Perhaps you've had somebody who lived before you the truth of God. Cherish the memories and apply the truths. Maybe you haven't. But you can become that person to someone you care about. You don't have to play at pretend prayer meetings; all you have to do is live your life of faith for your loved ones to see. Take them by the hand and lead them to spiritual safety.

*Jehovah, I'm glad I know you are the Creator. Jesus, I'm glad I know you are my Savior. Holy Spirit, I'm glad I know you are my Comforter. For those I love who do not know these truths, I pray for their awakening. And I ask you what part you would have me take in waking them up. Amen.*

# Uncle Brother

> I will turn their mourning into gladness;
> I will give them comfort and joy instead of sorrow.
> JEREMIAH 31:13

One of the most colorful people in my family is Uncle Lawrence Morris Jr., my mother's only brother. His nickname is Uncle Brother. At more than seventy years old, he tries to act and think like a springtime chicken. He's always talking about his girlfriend, but I don't think he really has one. At least no one in the family has seen any sign of her!

Sixteen years ago, I became Uncle Brother's legal guardian because he was termed a "chronic alcoholic." Although he had accepted Christ as a young man, Uncle Brother had lived like the devil. He admits he has had his share of booze and all that goes with it. When he reached the point that all he wanted was his drinking, someone had to care for him, and that someone turned out to be me. As his guardian, I made decisions he didn't agree with, but we couldn't deal with each other on level ground as one adult to another. It was a dark night in our relationship, and we didn't know if the morning would ever dawn.

But even when I was angry with him for the way he treated everyone, I prayed for him to return to the Lord. I prayed for the Holy Spirit to convict him and to give him no rest until he repented and started to live for God. I didn't want Uncle Brother to die without realizing he could enjoy a better life than the one he had chosen. He knew I loved him because I put up with him. And I often told him I loved him in spite of the way he responded to me after I said it.

Thanks be to God, we made it through that night; our sorrow turned to joy. Over the past several years, Uncle Brother has made some major changes. Now he talks about how God has brought him through dangers seen and unseen. He praises God in song. He watches Christian television. He reads his Bible. He bridles his tongue. He speaks affectionately about people. He has changed his friends. He is respected in his community. He is concerned about other family members. He attends family celebrations. He's fun to be around. His mourning has turned to gladness and so has everyone else's in the family.

With my uncle, weeping endured for about ten years, but God was always present. He never left Uncle Brother alone. And he was waiting for my uncle to reopen his heart.

We endured turbulence and turmoil as the norm for years. But today, my uncle can sing with me, "This joy we have, the world didn't give it and the world can't take it away!"

Are you dealing with someone whom you feel will never change? Do you vacillate between wishing he would change and just wanting him to leave you alone? Have you given up expecting good things from that person?

Nobody is so far from God that he can't get back to the Lord. Our responsibility is to keep knocking at God's door about that person, to keep believing God will answer our prayers. Thank God for what he will do. Patiently but expectantly wait on the Lord. Renew your hope!

*Lord, that you never give up on us is more consoling than I can express. Just to watch you move people from the pits of hell to the portholes of glory is overwhelming. Let me always remember that because you made us you can change us. Increase my patience with those who seem like hopeless causes. And renew my persistence in praying for them. Amen.*

# Jumping the Gun

Yet not my will, but yours be done.
LUKE 22:42

Have you ever watched runners during the Olympics preparing to start a race? They carefully position themselves in the starting blocks, placing their feet just so, and their hands on the ground in the way they have practiced for hours. Then, at the pop of the gun, they take off with everything in them.

But if one of the racers, too eager to get those mini-seconds of a head start, jumps out of the blocks before the gun sounds, a false start is declared, and everyone has to go through getting set in the blocks again. Sometimes a race can have two or three false starts. Everyone gets really tired, antsy, and irritable.

I've had a few false starts myself. At times I was so ready to rush out to grab God's will that I thought I heard the gun only to learn I'd jumped out of the blocks too soon. I remember one day writing down plans for a ministry building, furnishing it (in my mind), imagining the open house, and seeing the finished project before it began. I was set to leap out of those starting blocks.

Then a chance to purchase a building came up. And I was off! I believed God was saying, "This is it, kid." I believed I even heard God's voice (in my spirit) telling me to purchase things, as if I owned that building. I bought the curtains, cooking utensils, dishes, floral arrangements, and candles for this new place. I knew he meant *now*.

But my plans for that building never worked out. I sought every avenue to purchase it but experienced only drawbacks, setbacks, and obstacles—lots of false starts. But, I'm the obstacle-jumpin' lady. I've even written a book about it, I'm such an authority on the subject.

Finally, I became impatient and a little angry because of the obstacles. Then I had enough sense to ask God what was going on. I asked him to take the desire for this building out of my mind if this wasn't his will for me. Almost instantly, the desire for the building left. Ain't that somethin'? I was agonizing over a plan that wasn't in God's timing or will for me. I was acting on my own desires. Thank God he kept calling out, "False start!"

When I didn't get the building I thought I was supposed to have, I waited until December 1997 for God to grant me what he had promised me—four years before. Here's how it happened. The landlord for the structure I had been occupying told me he was going to increase the cost of the lease by more than fifty percent.

So several days after his announcement, I started to drive around looking for lease or rent signs. During my drive, the Holy Spirit asked me, "Why are you wasting time? I already have a building for you." I stopped looking, turned around, and went grocery shopping.

The following evening, I was talking to family members about my problem. One of them said, "You know, that house on Cedar Crest is still vacant." I contacted the proper people, and within three weeks, my office was relocated in a beautiful facility that God had prepared for us before the idea of a ministry building ever entered my mind. When the time was right, we were off and running.

Two impatient people in the Bible knew all about jumping the gun and the consequences that can bring. Remember Sister Sarah and Brother Abraham? God told the two of them they would have a child. But waiting for nearly a century got on Sarah's nerves. So she told Abraham to sleep with her handmaiden, Hagar.

Abraham didn't mention anything to Sarah about that being a false start. In fact, he didn't seem to have a problem with the idea at all. Hagar conceived a son, who by the customs of that day, became Sarah's property. But this wasn't a happy ending. Hagar, the natural mother, ridiculed Sarah because she couldn't have children.

Sarah grew irate and blamed Abraham for the trouble. She said, "You're responsible for the wrong I'm suffering."

Abraham, who was impatient himself, replied, "Do with her whatever you think best."

So Sarah mistreated Hagar, and Hagar ran away into the desert.

Now, God had told Abraham he would be the father of many nations. God's plan was to bless Sarah with a son. But Sarah was ninety and Abraham a hundred years old before their son, Isaac, was born. I admit, I probably would have gotten frustrated too. But a whole lot of suffering could have been alleviated if Sarah and Abraham hadn't jumped the gun, rushing on ahead of God.

Have you ever had a dream or a creative idea that you believed came from God? Since it came from God, he must be telling you to do it now, right? In your mind you're thinking, *Oh, what a good God! He expects me to use my intellect, academic competence, position, status, accomplishments to take control of this situation and get what I'm after. I'm a logical, analytical human being. I know what I'll do, I'll just . . .*

When we surrender our will to the Father, as Jesus did, we don't need to be concerned about how things will come out. God has promised the very best for us. Waiting is hard, I know. But false starts don't get us anywhere we want to go either.

*Father, as I try to do your will, I often jump the gun. Thank you for your patience toward me and your protection. I really don't mean any harm. When I start to edge off the racing block, keep me from moving out. Amen.*

# Harmony

Be joyful always; pray continually.
1 THESSALONIANS 5:16–17

If I had my druthers, when my three children were growing up, I would have shielded them from all trouble. For them I would have cut teeth, bumped my head, skinned my knees, fought their fights, taken their heartaches, healed their relationships, handled their finances, suffered their pains, and guarded them from disappointments.

But life's not like that. People have to endure their own situations. Evidently, none of those problems did irreparable damage to my children. They turned out just fine. As I think about what would have happened if I had taken on their hurts, I can't help but say, "They sure would have made some stupid adults!" And I've learned that I should take their hurts to someone who can do something about them.

I remember one time when Vikki was in college and called home confused about her self-worth and her relationship with God. The questions she asked were perplexing to me; I didn't have adequate answers.

My heart was hurting because I didn't know what to say that would give her the encouragement she needed. So I prayed something like this, "Lord, I don't know how to pray for my child. I don't even understand how she got to this point. She was always self-confident, strong, and sure of you. Help me to help her. Please tell me what to do, what to say, how to respond to her. Father, I feel helpless!" The prayer continued for I don't know how long.

When I finished, I opened my eyes and saw a book on the shelf in front of me. It was Zig Ziglar's *See You at the Top.* I took that book and mailed it to Vikki even though I hadn't even read all of it and, at the time, didn't remember much of it. But I mailed it anyway, thinking possibly God would use it in her life.

A few days later, my child called and said, "Mama, thank you for sending me that book. It has literally changed my life. All the questions I had were answered."

I couldn't fix her hurt, but I could take her hurt to the One who knew how to bring healing, and he did it through a method I would never have guessed.

I've had similar times of intense prayer for my son and my other daughter. As a mother, I find solace in praying for my children during the good times and the bad. It's a fact, when our children are hurt or disappointed, confused or sad, we hurt too. I think we feel their emotions as deeply as they do.

To help my children and myself to get focused on how to deal with problems, I ask my children if they have listened to praise music before they called to tell me about their woes. Sometimes they have; sometimes they haven't. If they haven't, I ask them to call back after they have — unless, of course, it's an emergency.

I believe one of the best ways to get in a praying mood is to listen to music that ushers you into a spirit of adoration. That, in turn, takes your mind off the problem and helps you to focus on the Problem Solver. It brings harmony to your soul.

While I wait for them to call back, I follow my own instructions. I sing, listen to gospel music, and pray. Usually, when they phone me again, both of us are in harmony with each other and the Lord.

We are admonished to pray without ceasing because prayers assert God's power in our lives. When we fail to pray, we aren't cheating God; we're cheating ourselves. I like the following prayer because it reminds me that I can pray about anything:

> Give me a good digestion, Lord,
> And also something to digest;
> Give me a healthy body, Lord,
> With sense to keep it at its best.
> Give me a healthy mind, Good Lord,
> To keep the good and pure in sight,
> Which, seeing sin, is not appalled
> But finds a way to set it right.
> Give me a mind that is not bored,
> That does not whimper, whine, or sigh;
> Don't let me worry over much
> About the fussy thing called "I."
> Give me a sense of humor, Lord,
> Give me the grace to see a joke,
> To get some pleasure out of life
> And pass it on to other folk.
>
> FROM THE REFECTORY OF THE CATHEDRAL
> AT CHESTER, ENGLAND

Shielding our loved ones from the consequences of their problems often isn't possible. But praying for their ability to handle those problems is appropriate and can benefit them and us. If you're trying to accept responsibility for the problems of others, pray for them and pray with them—without ceasing.

*Father, you've made it possible for us to stay in contact with you all the time, wherever we are. Even our unuttered thoughts can be prayers, which enables us to pray without ceasing. Thank you for always being available and never on vacation. Thank you, also, for allowing the Holy Spirit to pray for us when we don't know how to pray. Amen.*

# God's Mouthpiece

At the name of Jesus every knee should bow, in heaven
and on earth and under the earth, and every tongue confess
that Jesus Christ is Lord, to the glory of God the Father.

PHILIPPIANS 2:10–11

My husband, George, and I vacationed once with another couple in New Orleans. One day we spent four hours walking from the hotel to the end of the French Market, stopping to eat, shop, listen to jazz, watch a human mannequin, and observe the activities of this Cajun city.

After we had walked so far, all of us voted to take a taxi back to the hotel. So we flagged a cab. While the driver ate lunch and asked us where we were from, he drove us to our destination. His priorities seemed to be in that order: eat, talk, drive.

My friends told him they were from Houston, and George and I said we were from Dallas. The driver, in between bites of his sandwich, said, "I'm from Palestine. Do you know where Palestine is? It's where my people are fighting with the Jews because they have stolen our land."

His statements opened a path to an interesting and disturbing conversation. I asked him if the fighting over there was a continuation of the differences between Ishmael and Isaac. He replied, "No, the fighting started in 1948 when the Jews came back and stole our land."

"Do you think there will ever be peace in the Middle East?" I asked.

He replied, "Not until we kick them out and get our land back." He continued to explain about his people and their enemies, the Jews, and he moved on to crunching an apple.

The conversation then slid into a discussion of religion. He proudly told us he was a Muslim, and as a Muslim he believed in God. I wanted to know how he felt about Muhammad. He indicated Muhammad was a good guy just like Jesus. He didn't believe God had a Son. His reasoning was, "If God had one son, why didn't he have a daughter or a mother?"

That question didn't make sense to me, but I wasn't going to let that stop me from commenting. So I leapfrogged to a point I wanted to make. "Believing in Jesus happens in your heart by faith. I believe in Jesus Christ. I believe in the Trinity. What do you know about the Holy Spirit?"

Now it was his turn to be perplexed. Evidently he had never heard of the Holy Spirit. I was just warming up to the subject when, wouldn't you know it, we arrived at our hotel. Mr. Taxi Driver practically drove up on the curb and then opened the door with such energy, I thought it was going to come off the hinges. I wasn't sure if he was always that exuberant or if he was just happy to see this group of "Holy Spirit" people leaving his car.

Even after he dropped us off, my thoughts about the conversation continued. I rehearsed my statements and wondered what else I could have done to witness to the driver. What could I have said to show him that the way to get to God is through his only Son, Jesus? I realized I hadn't known enough about the Muslim religion to respond adequately to the issues Mr. T. Driver raised in our discussion. The more I thought about it, the heavier my heart became.

Then I remembered one of God's promises: that his Word would not return to him void. I could have used Scripture to help the Palestinian understand what I was saying. Several verses came to my mind even then.

Ultimately, I didn't gain perspective on that conversation until I reminded myself that if the fellow had accepted what I said and chose Jesus as his Savior right there in the taxi (hallelujah!), I couldn't have taken credit. God draws people to himself. Each of us is just his mouthpiece on earth.

Whether we say just the right thing or can't think of anything that seems right, all we can do is open our mouths and trust God to use us. That doesn't mean we shouldn't be prepared to offer a reasoned explanation for our faith, but it does take the pressure off of us. We are the instruments, but God is the one who must make the music through us.

After the taxi conversation, I asked God to forgive me for not adequately explaining who Jesus is. I asked God to speak to the driver's heart and to draw him to the Lord despite my muffed attempt. This prayer made me feel a lot better.

Have you tried to explain a spiritual principle to someone lately and sounded only sour notes? Have you been stymied about how to make clear that which seems so obvious to you? Remembering your role and God's role can help to comfort you if you've blown it and give you the push you may need to increase your knowledge so you can "sound off" more eloquently next time.

*Master, as one of your mouthpieces on this earth, I realize that sometimes you give me opportunities to talk about you that I blow. How grateful I am that when I miss my chance, you (I'm sure) have someone else you will use to draw that person to you. That doesn't get me off the hook, but it sure takes the pressure off. Teach me more about how to tell others about you. Amen.*

## My Shepherd

The LORD is my Shepherd, I shall not be in want.
PSALM 23:1

Most of the time when I say grace before a meal I say with conviction, "The LORD is my Shepherd, I shall not be in want!" Not because it's a short verse, which lets me feed my face sooner than saying a prayer, but because I really mean it.

When I say "The LORD is my Shepherd," I remember that he is my Savior, Master, Sovereign, All in All. He has charge over my life. As my Shepherd, he watches over me to see that I stay in the fold. He loves me unconditionally in spite of my going my own willful way sometimes. He protects me from danger. He provides everything for me. He chastises me when I do wrong. He comforts me when I am distressed. He bandages my wounds when I get hurt. He calms my fears when I am afraid. He takes care of my relationships when they become shaky. He bathes me in his Spirit when I seek his face. He communicates with me in ways I can understand.

"I shall not be in want." Now, that reminds me that I desire certain things: new draperies, new carpeting, new furniture. These are luxuries, not necessities, because I already have these things. I just want different ones. Know what I mean? God promises to provide all our *needs* according to his riches in glory in Christ Jesus (Phil. 4:19).

I know he will do that. And he delights in often giving us what we want as well.

I'm reminded of the time I wanted a government contract to financially sustain my speaking business. I prepared Requests for Proposals (RFPs) for almost a year. I thought there would be no end to all the paperwork and RRAs (Really Ridiculous Acronyms). After I submitted the proposals, months passed without a reply. I prayed, hoped, and waited, seemingly without an answer.

Finally, I called the office of one of the agencies and was told that they had decided not to do the programs. Then I received a letter indicating they had chosen someone else. Then I got an inquiry indicating they were resubmitting my request. I became disappointed and disillusioned with the governmental process. (Did I hear some "Amens"?) I wondered if the Good Shepherd had gone on vacation and left his sheep to wander—and wonder.

In retrospect now I see that the time I spent on the proposals and waiting for an answer was preparation for me to handle what God already had planned. You see, during the proposal writing time, I had to do a lot of research, compile a lot of training information, and do a lot of preparation that would never have occurred otherwise.

Finally, when God knew I was prepared to accept the challenges of my wants, he opened a door of opportunity and gave me a bigger and better contract with a private corporation that started an avalanche of new business in teaching cultural diversity. As the word spread about the success of the training and the benefits to corporations and governmental agencies, I began to receive calls from around the United States. For more than a decade, work rolled in. All the preparation paid off.

When I say, "The LORD is my Shepherd, I shall not be in want," it's more than just something to recite before eating. It's an affirmation that the Good Shepherd is watching over all the affairs of my life and is making sure I'm taken care of.

Have you been disappointed or disillusioned about something you wanted that God provided in a different way than you asked? Are you still waiting to hear a word from the Good Shepherd? (Which is a whole lot better than waiting for word from the government.) The next time you hear this verse, concentrate on the assurance that you can depend on him to watch over you, to protect you, to provide for you, to comfort you, to chastise you when you need it, to bandage your wounds, to calm your fears, to care for your relationships, to communicate with you, and to love you unconditionally. You shall not be in want.

*Thank you, Lord, for reassuring us that your powerful, providing hand will be extended to us in life's situations. Please help us not to take you for granted. We praise you as the Shepherd of our lives. Amen.*

# The Infamous Bra

Do not lie to each other, since you have taken off your old self
with its practices and have put on the new self, which is
being renewed in knowledge in the image of its Creator.
Here there is no Greek or Jew, circumcised or uncircumcised,
barbarian, Scythian, slave or free, but Christ is all, and is in all.

COLOSSIANS 3:9–11

Ladies come to the Women of Faith conferences with
all kinds of issues and situations. Some come with
their own agendas. And a few of them seem to be a little
over-the-top. You know, their compass seems to be
headed in the opposite direction from the rest of the
world.

That's the impression TJ gave at a conference
attended by fifteen thousand women earlier this year.
While other women were applauding the singers and
speakers, TJ waved a white, size 44D, lace brassiere in
the air, as high as she could.

She had come with a busload of ladies from her
church, but some of these fellow travelers were embarrassed by her unusual interaction with those on the stage.
Her pastor's wife vowed to take that thing away from TJ.
But she wasn't giving it up easily. Instead of handing over
the bra, she swirled it in the air and yelled "Hallelujah" at
the top of her voice. All her parish pals could do was act
as if they didn't know her.

I met TJ when she ran up to my book table during a break with the big bra in hand and enthusiastically insisted, "Sign my bra! Please sign my bra! I want you to sign it right here!"

I looked at her in shock. I have signed T-shirts, books, audiocassette and CD covers, brochures, programs, bumblebee pin cards, earring holders, postcards, and tablecloths. But bras, never. I thought, *If TJ has the nerve to sling a bra around in front of thousands of women and then ask me to autograph it, that's the least I can do.* I signed it, "My cup runneth over!"

Okay, so you think my compass is as misdirected as TJ's. I saw it all as great fun. TJ certainly seemed to be having a good time.

That autographing moment was the beginning of a wonderful relationship that has included spiritual growth and renewal for me. When I returned home from the conference, TJ telephoned and asked me to speak at her church for Multicultural Celebration Day. She said she had attended the Women of Faith conference asking God to direct her to the person the Lord wanted as speaker for the celebration day. She was convinced God had led her to ask me.

I agreed to be that speaker. During the many conversations with TJ that followed, I discovered she loves the Lord with all her heart. She has a passion for winning the lost to Christ and has compassion for hurting people. Her heartfelt urge for people to be united was evidenced by her consistent prayers for unity of the races, understanding among the denominations, and reconciliation of people's differences in every aspect of life. Her faith in God was evidenced by her determination to follow through on what she believed he had led her to do with this conference.

Sometimes TJ would call my answering service in the middle of the night to leave a word of encouragement for my staff and me to receive the following day. She introduced me to her mother and her husband over the telephone, and I recognized a family commitment to loyalty and harmony that could exist only among God-loving people.

The theme for the daylong celebration TJ organized was "Fresh oil — a new and fresh anointing uniting the body of Christ." And the day truly was a time of reconciliation for the body of Christ in that Methodist church in Arkansas. Along with learning to sing, "What a Friend We Have in Jesus" in Japanese, we were enlightened, encouraged, and inspired by representatives from Scotland, Russia, Puerto Rico, Mexico, Germany, Switzerland, Israel, Spain, Romania, Bulgaria, Korea, Poland, as well as by Native Americans and African Americans.

As the keynote speaker, I explained that every culture represented there had roots stemming from the flood survivors — Mr. and Mrs. Noah, Mr. and Mrs. Shem, Mr. and Mrs. Japheth, and Mr. and Mrs. Ham. But the most powerful time was after I spoke and the charge for reconciliation was given by TJ. We all sang, "Let there be peace on earth, and let it begin with me," as we went to each other with love, hugging and holding each other and saying words of apology or comfort. At that moment, all of us seemed to realize that we are sisters and brothers, valuable members of the human race regardless of origin or ethnic background.

Sharing communion was a beautiful sight. All the cultures represented were around the altar tearing pieces off a loaf of bread and dipping into the same cup of wine.

Just think, if I hadn't signed that infamous bra, I might have missed the opportunity to participate in the most prayed-up, planned-up, and thought-out day of cultural togetherness of my life. And I learned that not all people who act a little over-the-top should be labeled "offsides" just because they do things differently from the norm. You really can't judge a book by its cover. You have to look inside to see how the pages read.

Have you missed the opportunity of a lifetime because you thought the person who offered it was the sort who would use a size 44D bra as a flag? I'm not suggesting you throw caution to the wind. But I am suggesting that if someone presents you with an unusual opportunity, check your gut feeling before you write it off. God gave us intuition that can work for us when we let it. I don't suggest waving a brassiere at a conference, however. Leave that for TJ.

*Master, you did some unusual things during your walk here on earth. People thought you were a bit strange. Teach us to love everybody regardless of their race, ethnic origin, religion, geographic location, educational status, financial ability, social standing, personality, or physical ability. And when we want to ignore or move away from people we don't understand, help us to listen to our instincts and not to miss out on some of the best blessings—even when they come in unusual packages. Amen.*

# You-nique and Chosen

For you created my inmost being;
you knit me together in my mother's womb.
I praise you because I am fearfully and wonderfully made.

PSALM 139:13–14

God made you an original; don't die a copy. In the late seventies, a friend gave me a motto I use in all the sessions I present, whether Christian or secular: "In Christ, you can be the best of what and whom you want to BEE!" I also tell people about the bumblebee I wear every day, everywhere I go.

According to aeronautical science, the bumblebee can't fly. Its body is too heavy, and its wings are too shallow. But the bumblebee doesn't know it can't fly. So it flies around doing what God chose for it to do, pollinating plants. It does so without considering its limitations.

BEE aware that you too have talent, skill, aptitude, and ability that are you-niquely yours. No two people sing, dance, paint, speak, organize, manage, or teach just alike. When God made us, he made us special. We can be the best of what and who we want to BEE — and only God knows what our limitations are.

When I had my first child, I didn't understand about you-niqueness. So I tried to clone myself. I wanted to make my daughter in my image. But her personality was so different. She liked to stay in her room and read. She wasn't outgoing and didn't smile often. I thought she hated people. I would take her places and introduce her to people. Her response would be a cold, "Hi."

For years I put up with this attitude until one day it wore me down. I had introduced my twelve-year-old daughter to someone, and she gave her same non-nonchalant, nonpersonality, nonsmiling, unfriendly, "Hi." When we got back in the car, I verbally went for her jugular. I had a nervous breakdown on her for about forty-five minutes.

"What is wrong with you? Why are you so cold and nonresponsive? Why don't you act like you have home training? Do you hate people so much you don't even want to meet them?" I went on asking questions, and then I made another round in which I answered them myself.

When I finally finished my tirade, I noticed I hadn't moved her one bit. In fact, she just said, "Mama, I love you. But I'm not you. I don't even want to be like you."

What? Did she say she didn't want to be like me? What's wrong with me? How dare she; I'm a wonderful person. I decided to get my feelings hurt. (Notice I said, "I decided." Nobody can hurt your feelings without your cooperation.) I was so hurt I didn't even want to feed her, but I had to. After all, she was still my responsibility.

At first I couldn't rationally think about her comments. But, as I began to seriously consider what she was trying to communicate, I understood she was saying, "Mother, I am my own person. I have my unique personality and ask that you respect my individuality."

I started to pay more attention to her actions and discovered that reading, analyzing, and thinking through situations were things she was interested in. People were important, but more important to her were answers to questions she could find in books, magazines, and journals.

In fact, when I would take her to a grocery store or drugstore, she would stop at the magazine rack and would remain there until I was ready to leave. This very child has become the analytical, legal mind of my business. God made her unique.

If you have more than one child, you see the differences in them. We have three children. My middle child has my personality. He likes to make people laugh, obviously loves life, is a relational person. He also looks like his mother . . . a good-looking man! Our youngest child is more serious and quiet. She is patient, kind, tender, and compassionate.

When I disciplined child #1, she wanted to know: "Why? How many? How come? What do you mean by that?" And she expected clear-cut answers.

When I disciplined child #2, he would hug and kiss me and tell me he would never repeat the offense. Sure. Give him ten minutes, and he would be right back at it.

With child #3, all I had to do was look at her with motherly anger. She would start to cry because she never wanted to hurt or disappoint me.

Three different people with the same mother and father, but all unique and chosen by God.

You might appear to be different — or even strange — to some people. But remember, God made you in his image for his glory. Use your uniqueness to edify people and glorify God. Capitalize on the abilities God has given you. Don't expect other people to be like you or to always understand you. They're busy being uniquely themselves.

*Father, you make trillions of people, each with unique abilities, skills, thought patterns, talents, and personality. Each of us is different in so many ways. Thank you that our uniqueness can be linked to other people's uniqueness so harmony can exist in relationships, on our jobs, and in the church. Help us to accept other people's uniqueness as a God-given opportunity to blend and bless. Amen.*

## Tub Talk

The LORD is my strength and my shield;
my heart trusts in him, and I am helped.
My heart leaps for joy and I will give thanks to him in song.
PSALM 28:7

God and I have some of the most interesting conversations in the bathtub. Yes, I said "God and I." We talk to each other all the time. Some call it prayer or meditation. But, whatever works for you, we are talking in the tub.

I was praying that he would reveal to me how to explain his joy. Then I looked down at my hands splashing back and forth in the water, and I saw something I had never noticed before in that context—my diamond and gold jewelry.

On one hand I wore my platinum, antique, ornate, one-of-a-kind diamond and baguette wedding band, which had been on my finger for thirty-two years and had never needed repairing. I had enhanced it by adding a gold rope band to either side of it. On my pinkie finger, I noticed the small gold and diamond bumblebee that I have been wearing for more than ten years. And on that wrist I saw the gold bracelet my son made for me one Mother's Day. On my right hand was a gold and diamond bumblebee mounted on a wide gold band. This ring was a birthday present from my three children. All this jewelry is precious sentimentally as well as financially. And all of it has withstood time, remaining beautiful and sturdy. Just like joy, right, Jesus?

My eyes journeyed up my right arm to the scars resulting from the second- and third-degree burns I received when I dropped a deep fryer filled with boiling cooking oil one Fourth of July as I was frying fish for our family celebration. I don't fully recall the excruciating pain, but the scars remind me of the event. When I burned my arm, the jewelry I was wearing, even though saturated in hot oil, was just as valuable after the experience as before. Just like joy that comes through our fiery trials, right, Jesus?

I focused again on the tub water and I thought, *How often do I put my hands in water? Maybe twenty times a day? And I put my hands in all kinds of water because I travel so much. I don't know about the chemicals in that water, whether it be hard or soft, fluorinated or not.* Yet the water has not, in any way, destroyed my jewelry. Because the gold and diamonds are real, not counterfeit. Just like Jesus' joy.

A few years ago thieves broke into our home and stole some of my jewelry. Thank God, we recovered a great deal of it. When we got it back, the quality of the jewelry was the same as before. But, like many women, I have bags of costume jewelry — three dresser drawers' full, in fact. These bags contain little of monetary value; I just like the stuff. I can imagine that, if the thieves had grabbed some of that jewelry, they would have wanted to come back and toss the stuff in my face. The faux jewelry is counterfeit. It looks pretty for a while, but then it begins to fade, peel, and break. If you wear it in water long enough, it will turn your skin green. Of course, it would never make it through the hot oil.

Genuine versus counterfeit. Real versus fake. Long-lasting versus short-term. Joy versus happiness. The world didn't give me joy, and the world can't take it away. Joy gives me calm assurance even though I go through the valley of the shadow of death. Joy enables me to hold my peace when people say and do ugly things to me. When we go through troubles, afflictions, persecution, danger, illness, and distress, when the enemy comes to steal, kill, and destroy, we can have genuine joy in our hearts.

But one thing makes my jewelry very different from joy. The first time I was given a piece of fine jewelry, I was so excited I told my friends and a few of my enemies. I wanted everybody to know. But after I wore that jewelry for a short time, the thrill wore off, never to be regained.

Joy, on the other hand, is permanent. Once you have it, you never lose it. It may be overshadowed by human frailties, but real joy lasts for eternity.

*Father, I love our intimate conversations. You use symbols that we can identify with that help us understand you better. Draw to yourself those who haven't experienced your unspeakable, everlasting, abiding joy. Amen.*

# Pressing On—and
# We Ain't Talkin' Ironing

Not that I have already obtained all this, or have already
been made perfect, but I press on to take hold of that for
which Christ Jesus took hold of me.

PHILIPPIANS 3:12

Every time we pick up a newspaper or turn on the
news, we receive a plethora of bad news. The government's state of affairs isn't good. Shootings and mur-
der, abuse and abandonment continue. Storms lash
various parts of the country. Eating certain foods causes
disease; not eating others makes us susceptible.

Sometimes I take a break from the world of news. My
husband taunts me, saying, "It's a shame a woman of
your intelligence can't talk intelligently about current
affairs." Well, sometimes I choose to be ignorant.

A woman in the Bible was plagued with bad news, but
she decided that rather than tuning out, she would press
on. This woman's name was never given to us, but we do
know she had a lot of problems. She had been sick with
an issue of blood for twelve years. Apparently, this
woman, whom I've named Auntie Arlene because I feel
kinship with her sufferings, had been wealthy at one
time. But she had spent all her money trying to get well—
and hadn't seen any progress. If bankruptcy had been an

option in her day, she could have qualified. Her relationships were disbanded because of her defiled physical condition, and her disease was progressing.

I admire this woman for two reasons. First, when she heard Jesus was coming to her town, she was determined to see him. She believed that, if she could just touch his clothes, she would be healed. Second, this woman never gave up hope despite her years of anguish and disappointment. Her faith was bigger than a mustard seed. She believed Jesus would remove the mountain of desperation and desolation from her life.

As Jesus entered the town, a large crowd immediately gathered around him. Picture a bunch of ants discovering a picnic. They excitedly swarmed around him, pressing in as tightly as possible.

I can imagine all kinds of people milling about him, with a variety of motives for doing so. Some were curiosity seekers, others wanted to catch him breaking the Jewish customs, some were members of the council of the High Court, still others were criminals looking for pockets to pick, a number were people who believed Jesus was the Son of God. And you could also toss in an assortment of Pharisees, Sadducees, tax collectors, women, children, disciples, and those who are always eager to see the latest miracle being performed.

Among this eclectic group was a synagogue ruler, Jairus, who pleaded with Jesus to heal Jairus's dying daughter. Jesus started off on his emergency run to Jairus's home when Auntie Arlene pressed her way through the crushing crowd to touch Jesus' cloak. Immediately her bleeding stopped, and she realized she was freed from her suffering.

Jesus, realizing power had gone out from him, turned around in the crowd and asked, "Who touched my clothes?" Right. It was like someone noting he was brushed against while standing in a ten-person elevator containing thirty squished people.

But Jesus visually searched through the mishmash of the crowd, looking for who touched him. The woman fearfully pressed through the crowd, fell at his feet, and told him the whole truth. That would be like giving your doctor a report on your condition in front of a crowd—humiliating, scary, yet wonderful. Imagine her relief when Jesus replied, "Daughter, your faith has healed you. Go in peace and be freed from your suffering" (Mark 5:34).

Auntie Arlene had pressed on until she reached the source of her healing. She believed Jesus could help her. And she had faith and determination that nobody or nothing was going to stop her from getting what she needed from Jesus.

Because we live in a fallen world, we will experience negatives in our lives. Heartache and disappointment will come our way. We experience "stuff" we don't deserve, don't want, and can't send back. It's ours. But thanks be to God, nothing happens in this world that he doesn't know about and that he can't handle.

Auntie Arlene's story shows that, regardless of the hurts you experience in life, you know someone who has the power to take those negatives and turn them into positives. You know someone whose holy powers aren't hindered by the crowd, by anyone's hidden agenda, by fear, by doubt, by whining, by complaining, or by other people's opinions. Nothing can negate Jesus Christ's power to bring healing and peace.

Each time we encounter a trial, wouldn't it be a relief if we could concentrate on Jesus' ability to handle it, if we could keep pressing on until we regained peace—just like Auntie Arlene? Despite everything she had been through, she managed to keep hope alive.

Someone once told me, "Don't get your hopes up. All that does is set you up for a letdown." I disagree. If I don't keep my hopes up, where will they go? Romans 5:3–5 says, "Not only so, but we also rejoice in our sufferings, because we know that suffering produces perseverance; perseverance, character; and character, hope. And hope does not disappoint us, because God has poured out his love into our hearts by the Holy Spirit, whom he has given us."

*Oh, Lord, how awesome you are. Just one touch of your garment can make the most defiled clean. You know all about what we encounter every day. You know the negatives that surround us at home, work, school, church, in the community, and in our minds. Please remind us that if we continue to press toward you without giving up, you will surely heal and deliver us from our anguish. Help us to encourage others to lean on you when they seem discouraged by this world's troubles. Let us be an example by seeking comfort and peace in Jesus' presence. For in his presence is joy beyond measure. Amen.*

# A Song in Her Heart

The LORD your God is with you, he is mighty to save.
He will take great delight in you, he will quiet you with
his love, he will rejoice over you with singing.
ZEPHANIAH 3:17

Our family enjoys good gospel music. We have discovered that praising God in song lifts our spirits, clears our heads, and opens a place for the Holy Spirit to speak to us.

Alaya, my one-and-a-half-year-old granddaughter, is always singing. From the moment she could utter sounds, she made music. When her mother, Lesa, secured newborn Alaya in her car seat, this child would make sounds. As she developed, those sounds were easily recognizable as tunes such as the Barney song, the ABC song, "Jesus Loves Me," "Row, Row, Row Your Boat," and "Jesus Loves the Little Children."

Alaya sings when she is eating, having her diaper changed, playing, standing, pulling up, watching television, bouncing in her swing, sitting in a car, attending church. Everywhere, all the time, she has a song in her heart.

At first I wondered how she kept the sweetness, calmness, contentment, and joyfulness of singing all the time. But as I thought about it, I decided Alaya has loving parents whom she can depend on to take care of her, comfortable and safe surroundings to live in, little responsibility, a love of singing, lots of attention when she sings, and joy because in her little heart she feels God's love.

Just as Alaya feels secure and loved, God offers the same to his children. He extends care to us by meeting our every need (Phil. 4:19) and comforting us when we go through trials (Ps. 23:4). He tells us to put our cares on him because he is responsible for our existence and future (1 Peter 5:6–7), he stands ready to reveal to us truths about his Word (2 Tim. 2:15), and he loves us so much he sacrificed his Son to save us from eternal damnation (John 3:16).

Realizing all this, don't you think we have something to sing about? When you're going through your daily routine or when you face trials and tribulations, do you allow music to comfort you? When times are good, do you stop to sing for joy?

God enjoys the song we lift up in praise to him. He even reciprocates by singing back to us, as the verse in Zephaniah tells us, "He will rejoice over you with singing."

Just think, when we sing praises down here on earth, angels are singing around God's throne twenty-four hours a day, seven days a week: "Holy, holy, holy, Lord God Almighty, the earth is full of your glory." And we'll be joining them. An old Negro spiritual says, "If you miss me from singing down here and you can't find me nowhere, come on up to bright glory. I'll be singing up there."

Want to lift your spirits from the hustle and bustle of the day? Sing to the Lord. When praises go up, blessings come down. Now, isn't that something to sing about?

*Master of music and all good things, I adore you. You create a melody of sweet singing in the hearts of those who love you. Even if we can't sing melodiously, we can sing for joy at the works of your hands. We can praise you in the morning, afternoon, evening, and the midnight hour. And you sing back to us. What a promise! Thank you that melodies linger on in our hearts long after our voices have given way. We appreciate that it's not the sound of our voices that moves you but the condition of our hearts. Amen.*

## The Main Line

This is the confidence we have in approaching God:
that if we ask anything according to his will, he hears us.
1 JOHN 5:14

On a beautiful April day in Dallas, I was soaking in the refreshing sun rays. The temperature was a comfortable eighty degrees, and the breeze softly surrounded my shoulders as if God were cradling me in his arms. Birds were chirping in the background. Our front lawn was a splendid carpet of green, topped by two magnificent, thirty-year-old magnolia trees. As I looked up toward the heavens, not a cloud was in the sky.

But then something grabbed my attention. About forty feet above the carpet of grass were lines of cable wires laced together in conduits swagged from tall poles. The network of wire connected to other cables on other poles and to houses and more poles and houses . . . I hadn't noticed all this circuitry before.

As I thought about it, I realized these masses of wires make it possible for us to talk with our friends via telephone, e-mail, fax, and telegraph. Because of these lines, we could have money wired to my bank account. We could receive instant news about peace treaties and the weather as it happens. We have access to college studies and home decorating, cooking and remodeling, the symphony and the theater—all through these wires that criss-cross themselves from one pole to another.

But then I thought, *What happens when it storms, and these cables are down? We can't call for help. We can't send a message to anyone. We feel out of control and isolated. What we have taken for granted is no longer a source of contact for us.*

An old Negro spiritual reminds us of the most important connection we can make.

> *Jesus is on the main line.*
> *Tell him what you want.*
> *Jesus is on the main line.*
> *Tell him what you want.*
> *Jesus is on the main line.*
> *Tell him what you want.*
> *Call him up and tell him what you want.*

Have you ever attempted to get in touch with God and found yourself doubting his ability to help you? Do you find yourself worrying about things you should tell God about instead? Do you feel ashamed to talk to God? Do you find yourself seeking other people's opinions rather than relying on God's guidance? Do you think you have to use a certain posture or language to get God's attention? Do you think you've done something so awful you can't tell God?

If your answer is "yes" to any of those questions, you're creating unnecessary interference between you and God. Nothing can keep you from being directly connected to God if you want to be.

It doesn't matter what time of day or night it is, what day of the week it is, who else is talking to him, or what the problem is. He is always available to listen and to help us without static or interference. His omnipotence has blocked out anything and everything that would keep him from hearing and answering us.

When you need to make decisions and nobody on earth understands, call him up.

When your problems seem unbearable, call him up.

When you want to praise him and show appreciation for his wonderful work in your life, call him up.

When you want to communicate with someone who wants to communicate with you and who has all the answers to your questions, call him up.

It doesn't matter if the telephone lines are down all over the world, God is always available. The only interference that can hinder our communication is our rebellion and disobedience. Even then, he is ready and willing to forgive us and to accept our call. He's always near to comfort and cheer just when we need him most.

*God, sometimes I create interference when I'm trying to get to you. Maybe my faith is shaken or I have pouts or doubts. I don't try to contact you when I need direction because I try to do it myself. Sometimes I neglect togetherness with you because I'm lazy or just don't feel like it. What a consolation to know I'm the problem, not you. Thank you for always keeping your communication line open. Your listening ear is my source of comfort. Amen.*

## *No Coincidences*

Direct my footsteps according to your word.
PSALM 119:133

I'm amazed at the number of situations that seem to be coincidences — until I stop and take a look at the whole picture. For instance, I never thought of myself as an author until a set of circumstances started the pages to roll off the presses.

One of my business associates, without my knowledge, recommended me as a speaker for a national organization. I found out about it when the conference coordinator called to tell me I had been selected. When the time neared that I was to speak, the organization called my office and asked that my books be at the conference by a certain date.

"My books? Did she say, 'My books'?" I spouted to anyone who was within hearing. "I don't have *one* book, let alone *books*. Nobody told me you were supposed to be published to speak for this group. They want 'my books' in six weeks!"

My daughter Vikki was in the office at the time and immediately took the telephone from me. She wrote down the instructions on where the books should be delivered, agreed that I would have a book there on or before the date, hung up the phone, and handed me one of the greatest challenges of my life. "Write the book!" she said. "You know you have all the information you need. It's time to stop procrastinating and do it. You'll write on the plane, in your hotel room, everywhere you can. Send the information back to me and don't worry about the rest. You *will* have a book at the conference. You can do it; I know you can! Now, get on it!"

With Vikki's tenacity, my knowledge and determination, the help of other people who assisted on the project, and God's grace, the book was delivered by the required date. But this was no coincidence. God had placed the material for the book in my mind and heart several years before; the speaking engagement just prodded me to do the writing. God had lined up all the circumstances to make it happen. That was just the beginning, however.

The very day I released this first book, *Capture Your Audience Through Storytelling,* another publisher approached me about writing my second book. I was startled. Write another book? I didn't think I had anything else to say. The publisher said, "I want you to write about the challenges and triumphs of your life."

Challenges and triumphs of my life? Who would want to hear about my life? He said he wanted me to write something Oprah would buy. Well, the thought was worth entertaining. So off I went into the world of book writing once again, with my daughter pushing and prodding me all the way. With the help of Jan Winebrenner, a wonderful writer, within eighteen months the second book, *Bumblebees Fly Anyway: Defying the Odds at Work and Home,* was released. No coincidence!

One of the administrators at New Life Clinics read the book and was convinced I needed to be a Women of Faith speaker—me, a person she had never met or heard of. When she approached me about speaking, the dates of the conferences were open on my calendar. No coincidence! As a result of being a speaker for this marvelous organization, I have written another book released March 1998, *God Will Make a Way*.

I was fifty-two years old when I wrote my first book. Now, at fifty-seven, I have either written or coauthored six books. This writing frenzy all started with a friend suggesting me as a speaker for a conference. And the "coincidences" go on.

I was standing in line with two friends to board an airplane in Salt Lake City when a lady and her daughter noticed my purple and white Women of Faith tote bag. The mother asked if we had attended a conference, adding that they had been to one in Lakeland, Florida, the previous year.

"We've been trying to contact one of the speakers," she said. Then she looked at me and said, "The bee! The bee! You're the one! You're the one with the bumblebee pins! You're the one we've been trying to locate for more than three weeks!"

Would you believe the mother and daughter's seats on the plane were two seats from ours?

As you look back over the circumstances of your life, can you discern the carefully planned patterns that at first looked like coincidences? Situations don't always follow our plans, but God orchestrates our lives nonetheless—sometimes to a tune we hear only faintly.

*Help me, Lord, to relinquish my life to you. Be Lord over my career, family, friends, talents, skills, abilities, ideas, desires, and prosperity. Enable me to remember that you have ordered my steps and that you will bring to pass what you have planned. As I survey my life, keep me mindful that, while I'm amazed at what you have done, in many ways, you have just begun. Amen.*

# I Said I Was Sorry!

For I will forgive their wickedness
and will remember their sins no more.
JEREMIAH 31:34

When my two-and-a-half-year-old granddaughter,
Vanessa, visited my home recently, she was having
such a good time she forgot to mention she needed to use
the potty. Her mother, aunts, cousin, and grandmother
could see into the kitchen where Vanessa was industri-
ously playing. Most of us noticed the same thing at the
same time.

Vanessa was standing with a look on her face that said,
"Oh, oh, I'm going to catch it now!"

Tina, her mother, looked at Vanessa and exclaimed,
"What did you do?"

Vanessa answered with the angelic innocence of a
child, "I'm sorry."

"Vanessa, I thought I told you to tell me when you
want to use the bathroom. You're too special to be wet-
ting on yourself."

While Tina continued to fuss, Vanessa, a fifty-pound,
round mulatto with Shirley Temple curls swirling on her
head, again sweetly said, "I'm sorry!"

That didn't seem to faze her mother. She kept on fussing. "Vanessa, I don't understand how you can be so good

when we're at home, but as soon as we go somewhere, you forget to tell me." On and on she lectured.

Eventually, Vanessa grew sick of the endless discussion of her behavior. She was standing in a puddle, and her panties were wet. Everybody was looking at her and listening to Tina go on. So Vanessa widened her brown eyes, put her right hand where her hip would be if she had a waistline, slightly bent her left knee, and said to her mother with all the disgust of a disgruntled ten-year-old, "I *said,* 'I'm sorry!'"

Oh, my goodness. All of us were trying not to laugh. We had compassion for Vanessa's dilemma, but she had broken the rules.

How often do we ignore God's rules for our lives because we're too busy, we're too involved in our own thing, we don't believe, we make up our own rules, or we choose to be downright rebellious? I can imagine God looking at us something like Tina looked at Vanessa and saying, "My child, how many times does it take to convince you that my way is the right way? My timing is the perfect timing? My authority is the ultimate authority? My instructions will lead you to a way that has been designed for your good. Why don't you obey me?"

As he questions us, if we're sensitive to listen to his admonishment, we're quick to say, "Father, I'm sorry!" Before the twinkling of an eye, he says, "Forgiven!"

Hallelujah, we don't have to listen to all that fussing! He knows when we mean what we say and when we don't. He is ready, willing, and able to forgive to the utmost without continuing to talk and talk and talk. Praise God for the power in the phrase, "I'm sorry!"

Do you and God need to have a little talk? I promise you it will be short if you go to him with a humble heart, saddened by your sin.

*Father God, I appreciate that when we fail to obey your rules and tell you how sorry we are, you listen with compassion and forgive us. Oh, what grace! Please accept my apology for the many times I have defied your authority and haven't followed the rules. Thank you for allowing us to say, "I'm sorry." Amen.*

## *Payday*

The man who plants and
the man who waters have one purpose,
and each will be rewarded
according to his own labor.

1 CORINTHIANS 3:8

One of the sweet benefits of speaking for the Women of Faith conferences is receiving a candy bar. Often, but not always, Mary Graham, the program coordinator, gives each speaker a Payday candy bar for keeping her presentation within the allotted time. Sometimes she gives us one just because she cares.

I think she's smart not to hand them out each conference because we've begun to expect them. We're like little children. We ooh and aah over our Paydays more than we do our paychecks—well, almost more. Getting that candy bar with "Payday" written on the wrapper ignites a spark of joy in us.

I wonder how it will be when we Christians are around Christ's judgment seat, and he's looking over our record at the assignments he has given us while we were on earth. He will be handing out Paydays too. Well, actually he calls them "crowns" or "rewards." Five crowns will be available to us if we've followed his orders. Five crowns? Yes! And I want all of them.

True, no amount of work will enable you to inherit eternal life. The plan of salvation is simply to believe Jesus is Lord and that God raised him from the dead. Salvation is a gift.

But works count for something. Ain't that good news! James 1:12 says, "Blessed is the man who perseveres under trial, because when he has stood the test, he will receive the *crown of life* that God has promised to those who love him" (emphasis mine).

"Do you not know that in a race all the runners run, but only one gets the prize? ... Everyone who competes in the games goes into strict training. They do it to get a crown that will not last; but we do it to get a *crown that will last forever* [an imperishable crown]" (1 Cor. 9:24–25).

"For what is our hope, our joy, or the *crown in which we will glory in the presence of our Lord Jesus* [a crown of exultation] when he comes? Is it not you? Indeed, you are our glory and joy" (1 Thess. 2:19–20).

"But you, keep your head in all situations, endure hardship, do the work of an evangelist, discharge all the duties of your ministry. For I am already being poured out like a drink offering, and the time has come for my departure. I have fought the good fight, I have finished the race, I have kept the faith. Now there is in store for me the *crown of righteousness*, which the Lord, the righteous Judge, will award to me on that day—and not only to me, but also to all who have longed for his appearing" (2 Tim. 4:5–8).

"Be shepherds of God's flock that is under your care, serving as overseers—not because you must, but because you are willing, as God wants you to be; not greedy for money, but eager to serve; not lording it over those entrusted to you, but being examples to the flock. And when the Chief Shepherd appears, you will receive the *crown of glory* that will never fade away" (1 Peter 5:2–4). (This crown is not just for pastors but for all those who are faithful to whatever ministry God has called them.)

I'm excited just thinking about that pageant of crowns I can qualify for if I work the works of him who sent me. Just like speaking at the Women of Faith conferences. I work because I know God has placed me there, not to receive that Payday candy bar. But when Mary hands me that sweet slab, I cherish it. In a much deeper way, I will cherish that last chance to be rewarded for a life well spent when I receive my rewards in heaven.

Do you like to receive gifts? Maybe nobody will recognize your works on earth, but God will never forget what you've done for him. He sees your heart and knows your motives. You too can look forward to your Payday in heaven.

*Father, I'm amazed to think that you will judge us Christians for things we've done for you. If our works are genuine, they are made of gold, silver, and precious stones. If not, they are like wood, hay, straw. Gracious Lord, sometimes I'm negligent and don't even think about the good I could do—not to be rewarded but because you knew it would satisfy my longing to participate in life. Please, Lord, accept my apology for not always following your instructions. Help me to remember that you have many crowns to set on my head in the hereafter, but keep me mindful of doing good not for payday but for you. Amen.*

## *Firsthand Knowledge*

No temptation has seized you except what is common to man.
And God is faithful; he will not let you be tempted
beyond what you can bear. But when you are tempted,
he will also provide a way out so that you can stand up under it.

1 CORINTHIANS 10:13

In March 1998, Luci and I spoke at a church conference near Dallas with the theme of friendship. Luci spoke on friendships with others. I was asked to speak on friendship with Jesus. At first I thought, *This is a breeze.* Then I started to figure out how to approach the subject.

I asked God to give me what he wanted me to say. Nothing happened. The time drew nearer, and I kept thinking and thinking, jotting down ideas, trying to get it together. Nothing made sense. The afternoon before the conference, still nothing had come. About 9:30 the night before, God came through. (Why can't he be early sometimes?) This is what occurred to me.

Have you ever considered that Jesus the God-man experienced everything we humans experience? I can see him as a baby crying, kicking, scooting, crawling, pulling up, learning how to eat and walk just like an ordinary baby. As a little toddler, Jesus played and got dirty. Mary and Joseph would tell him to stop doing little toddler things and try to get him to put his food in his mouth—and leave it there.

I can see Jesus' earthly father instructing him in carpentry. I can imagine Jesus playing outside with the neighborhood kids and his parents telling him to come inside at a certain time. When Jesus got left behind in Jerusalem, I can imagine Mary, after missing him, saying to the other children, "Have you all seen Jesus? I thought he was walking with you. You mean none of you has seen him since we left the temple? Oh, my goodness, we have to go back and find that boy." They, of course, found him in the temple going about his Father's business.

Can't you see him at mealtime listening attentively to Jewish history and learning Jewish customs? Parents were to teach their children in the morning, afternoon, evening, and night. As the older people discussed the Law, can't you just see this inquisitive boy straining his ears to hear every word?

He had the same physical needs that we have. He got hungry and thirsty. He grew tired and needed to rest and go on vacation like we do. He showed emotions. He wept and became angry and disgusted. He enjoyed a good party. He motivated crowds of people. He enjoyed recreation. He was tested. He understood fear and sadness. He was surrounded with rebellion and death. He dealt with sickness and disease. He was unacknowledged in his hometown. He was ridiculed and talked about, lied to and left out. He was falsely accused and abused and experienced prejudice. He was humiliated, beaten, and killed.

Jesus is the only friend who understands everything that can happen to us. He knows firsthand how situations feel, taste, smell, sound, hurt, tempt, disappoint, excite, motivate, influence, stimulate ... everything. We can feebly try to tell him about our experiences, but he already knows, sees, and understands.

A favorite hymn of mine says:

Jesus is all the world to me.
My life. My joy. My all.
He is my strength from day to day.
Without him I would fall.
When I am sad, to him I go.
No other one can cheer me so.
When I am sad
He makes me glad.
He's my friend.

*Jesus, you experienced the good, the bad, and the ugly. A thought can't even slip through my mind that you haven't already known. You see the before, during, and after of every event. When I think that you physically, mentally, and spiritually tasted all of my experiences, it's easier for me to rely on you for direction, clarity, instruction, healing, emotional stability, spiritual growth, and wisdom. Thank you, Jesus, for being my friend. Amen.*

# This Is the Lord's Day

This is the day the LORD has made;
let us rejoice and be glad in it.
PSALM 118:24

Each day the Lord gives us brings with it reasons to rejoice.

When my husband says, "Baby, you need to go buy two or three suits," I take delight in his care for me. When my grandbaby strikes up a conversation with me — "Hey, Grammy: love you! Bye" — it brings joy to my heart. When my kids come over every Sunday and my grandkids mess up my house, leaving their little dirty socks lying around, smearing their fingerprints on my glassware, I feel pleasure. I wake up the next morning and laugh. I look at my windows — and of course my house has just been cleaned — and there are fingerprints from the little fingers that had candy all over them. I look in my bathroom mirror, and know that somebody had to climb up on the counter and put those little sticky hands on the mirror. Joy just leaps in my spirit.

When I get a thank-you card from an employee or a nice smile from one who says, "I like my job," I receive it as a gift from the Lord. I feel his care when someone gives me a gift that is precious to her heart or when my friend Barbara Johnson calls me up and says, "Hello. Whatcha doing? Just want to see what's going on." I know he is speaking to me when a lady on our mailing list e-mails me a different Scripture passage each day.

Sometimes the day holds surprising gifts in store. The other day I went to film a segment for a television series I'm on with a Dallas station. This is not a Christian station. But when I arrived for the session, the producer and the executive producer both asked me to pray with them. It turns out they are Christians. We prayed for the program and for the viewers who were going to see it that day—right on the set, in front of the crew. This is highly unusual for secular television, and it brought joy to me.

Rejoice in this day the Lord has given to you. He has joy waiting for you.

*This day, Lord: Open my eyes to the blessings you have in store for me. Thank you for a new chance to see you at work and to give you praise. Amen.*

## Overcoming Distractions

What gets in the way of my ability to live in the moment is trying to do too many things at once, forgetting that if I just pick up the first thing first and the second thing next, I'll get things done I have to get done. Instead I tend to start feeling cluttered or panicked that I can't possibly finish it all, and I don't get *anything* done right until I slow down long enough to focus on one task at a time.

For example, I have photographs in a four-drawer chest of drawers. Do you understand I'm saying *four drawers?* Someday before I die, I'm going to take a week off and put them in the photo albums I have already purchased.

Sometimes my clutter piles up when I procrastinate on tasks I wish I didn't have to do: exercise, for instance. I'm working on not hating it. I don't hate the exercise; I just resent that I have to give time to it. Once I do it, I feel good. What's hard is choosing to do that instead of something else I think I need to accomplish.

I tend to be bothered most by internal distractions. The best way I've found to overcome them is to get up early enough in the morning to get the things out of the way I don't really want to do. Then they don't take up space in my mental bank all day. I do the worst first so I can put it behind me.

The most wonderful truth behind dealing with distractions is that we don't need to organize and plan with our natural ability alone. The Holy Spirit, who gives us everything we need, can lengthen or shorten time depending on what he wants us to accomplish. If we yield ourselves to him, he will order our steps according to his purposes.

*This day, Lord, keep me from becoming overwhelmed by demands and distractions. Help me to clear away mental clutter and focus on those things that are important to you. Then give me grace to do them well. Amen.*

# *Dealing with Anxiety*

Nothing gets in the way of enjoying everyday gifts like anxiety. The two Scriptures I most often turn to in order to help me deal with anxiety are Jeremiah 29:11 and Philippians 4:5–6.

As you enter my house, right across from the front door you'll see a big plaque on the wall. It's parchment with gold letters that read, "'I know the plans I have for you,' says the Lord. 'Plans for your well-being, and not calamity. Plans to give you a future and a hope.'" When my day gets hectic and things aren't working the way they're supposed to, or when my children's lives are in turmoil, I go back to this passage: *Now, what did he say?*

In Paul's counsel to the Philippians for overcoming anxiety, he reminds them first that God is with them (v. 5). Then he instructs them to pray and ask and give thanks in all things. The God who is with them is a God of peace, and his peace will rule in their hearts and minds. Now I've had to wrestle with these truths many, many times. When I grow anxious about what is required of me, I go back to this passage. When somebody calls me with bad news, or my kids call me with problems they're facing, I go back to this passage. *What does the Word say?* Don't worry about it. Be anxious for nothing. Why shouldn't we worry about it? Because worry says to God, "Lord, I don't trust you."

But we *do* worry, and then what? With prayer and supplication, we thank God for giving us this talk again. We thank him for the process he is taking us through. Not that we want it, but because we know we're going to be the better for having gone through it. We thank him that we're not parked in there; we're not stuck. We're going *through.*

And then what does he do? He keeps his promise. He gives us peace. We don't understand it, it doesn't make sense, it's crazy, but he gives us peace we cannot comprehend — peace not only in our minds but also in our hearts. That is outrageous. That is supernatural.

These are the truths I cling to when my day is disrupted by anxious thoughts. "Cast all your care upon Him," Peter tells us, "for He cares for you" (1 Peter 5:7 NKJV). There is no better place to go.

*This day, Lord, I cast my cares upon you, for I know that you care for me. You do not want me to be anxious about anything. Keep me in your perfect peace. Amen.*

# *Don't Go It Alone*

While I was growing up, I had many difficult experiences, but I was always surrounded by believers. I've talked a lot about my granny (my great-grandmother), who raised me in the fear of the Lord. I remember her coming to hear me sing the lead part in an elementary school play when I was six or seven. She was an active participant in my school activities and an officer in the PTA. The first day of school she brought me in and said to the instructor, "Listen: this is a child; you are the teacher. I expect you to teach her; I expect you to discipline her; and if there's something you can't do with her, then I expect you to let me know!" Then she turned to me: "Do you understand that, Thelma?" Many a day she would come to school, even into my high school years. Her active presence in my life was a great joy to me.

My granddaddy (Granny's son) balanced out my mean grandmother. He would take me to the Majestic Theater in downtown Dallas. Because we were black, we had to sit in the buzzard roost, but still I loved to go. He also took me to parties, and he would let me ride the train through downtown Dallas. He worked on the railroad, and he would put me on the back of the train while he took his spot up front. I never knew that, however, so I'd always be wondering how in the world he could be waiting for me on the platform at the next station when I had just seen him waving good-bye to me on the last one!

My uncle and aunt, James and Allene Morris, taught me social graces. They would take me to dinner at the only fine restaurant black people could go to in Dallas, the Shalomar. They taught me how to use my napkin, where the salad fork and dinner forks go, the difference between the butter knife and the steak knife, and how to care for silver, crystal, and china. Consequently, when Allene died, she left me all her crystal and silver as well as a china cabinet to keep it in.

These godly people taught me a lot about life. They were examples to me of the love of God. I was also surrounded by believers in our church who modeled to me what God was like and taught me lessons from Scripture. Everywhere I went, there were glimpses confirming that God was real. Each summer until I was eighteen, I went to girls' camp for two weeks. I saw God in the teachers. I would drink springwater coming from the rock. I would put my little tin cup under the springwater coming from rocks in a stream, and it was so cold and fresh, I knew in my spirit that only God could purify the water running down a rock.

If you have days when you wonder where God is showing up, think about the believers he has placed in your life to influence you in a godly way. Give him thanks for these evidences of his work in your life. Godly friends are one of God's simple gifts to us.

*This day, Lord, thank you for the believers in my life who have testified to your goodness. Show me how to bring to others the blessings I have received from these dear brothers and sisters in Christ. Amen.*

## I Will Fear No Evil

**M**y ability to embrace life each day without being afraid of what might happen is rooted in a childhood experience that helped to affirm for me God's goodness. When I was a child, I suffered from many fears. I had a lot of nightmares. I was afraid a lot of the time. Daddy Harrell was blind, but he noticed the fear in me. People would come up to me, and I'd scream.

One day he said to me, "Pooch, come here to this bed." It was a rollaway bed on our back-alley upstairs apartment with a screened-in porch. "Sit down," he said. "There's a way you can be free of your fear, but you're gonna have to do what I tell you. If you want to get rid of being afraid all the time, you got to close your eyes, lay down on this bed, and say the Lord's Prayer and the Twenty-third Psalm over and over, one behind the other, until you don't feel scared no more."

I trusted him so I laid down and said those prayers over and over. When I opened my eyes again, through the screen of that porch I saw the clouds up in the sky forming the bust of Jesus, and he was smiling. From that moment until this day, for more than fifty years, I have not been afraid again. I have traveled all over the world—including from Dallas to London during Desert Storm—and I have never been afraid.

Are you facing fears this day? Do they keep you from recognizing the goodness of God in your life? Then I would encourage you today to pray the Lord's Prayer and Psalm 23 over and over until you feel the Lord lifting from you the burden of your fear. If you are busy and distracted by demands, then take this short prayer with you and pray it without ceasing: "I will fear no evil, for you are with me" (Ps. 23:4).

*This day, Lord, speak to me in the prayers I offer from your Word. Quiet my fears by the assurance of your presence. Amen.*

## Yes, I Believe!

Scripture is filled with encouragement for our faith because we are so vulnerable to doubt and fear when we feel overwhelmed by life. Many of us have difficulty celebrating each day as a gift from the Lord because stress is coming at us from umpteen different directions. The more confidence we have that he is active in our lives, the more we will turn toward him rather than away from him when we are stressed to the max.

We acquire this confidence gradually, across a lifetime of placing our trust in God and finding out each time that he is faithful. Over the years my prayers have changed as I continue to go through more and more adventures that show me God is at work in my life. As I look back on my early years, I recall several experiences in which the reality of God's presence in my life became very vivid. These "Yes, I believe!" encounters have stayed with me ever since, nurturing and strengthening my faith.

One of the joys of my life is remembering how Dr. Ernest Coble Estell Sr. held me up in his arms and baptized me when I was four years old. He was holding me way up high because I was just a little thing. I had on a white baptismal robe, and all the lights in the church were off except the one over the baptistery. There was a picture behind us of John the Baptist baptizing Jesus, and a dove coming down out of heaven. I remember hearing the organist of our church playing, "Wade in the water;

wade in the water . . . God's going to trouble the water." I heard Reverend Estell ask me, "Do you believe Jesus Christ is the Son of God?" And I said, "Yes." I can see this so clearly in my mind's eye: my first act of submission to God. Ever since, I have considered the ordinance of baptism so sacred that I don't think people ought to *move* when someone is being baptized.

When I was in kindergarten, I heard two dear women, Thelma Walker and Thelma Wilson, talk about how Jesus loves the little children. I heard those women talking about how Jesus wanted the little children to come to him and about all we had to do was say, "Jesus, come into my heart," and I knew that Jesus wanted me. I knew that he had come into my heart.

As an eighteen-year-old, during the Easter season, I attended an extraordinary service in which an artist came to our church. Using iridescent crayons that glowed in the dark, he drew the crucifixion. I was sitting in the balcony of the darkened church, listening intently as the artist told the story of the crucifixion while he was drawing. When he reached the description of Jesus' blood dripping from the crown of thorns on his head and flowing from the nail prints in his hands and feet, the blood became real to me. I remember standing up and shouting in exuberance that God was our Father, Jesus was the Savior, the Holy Spirit the Comforter.

Twice God gave me this deep assurance of his saving presence: once as a little girl, when he delivered me from all my fears, and when he confirmed to me by the power of an artist's rendition that our God reigns, that he is the Lord, that this was not a sham. Salvation was real through the blood of Jesus.

When daily living plagues you with questions about what God is up to in your life, recall how he has made himself known to you in the past. Thank him for drawing you to belief in him through these experiences. Allow them to restore your confidence in the God who never changes.

*This day, Lord, help me in my weakness and doubt. Strengthen my faith through bringing to remembrance those significant moments in my life when your Spirit prompted me to affirm, "Yes, I believe!" Amen.*

## Rejoice in This Day

Every day we must renew our minds. I don't think God means do not plan, do not look forward to days to come. I believe he means that right now is the only opportunity we have to live for him. Treat this moment, right now, as if it's your last moment because it might be. Yesterday's blessings and progress are not today's. Be kind *today*. Lift up the Lord *today*. Share something with someone *today*.

Jesus taught us to pray, "Give us this day our daily bread." Each day we have to eat. Yesterday's meal will not tide us over. Every day has its own agenda, its own blessings, its own challenges and triumphs. Live in the moment *now*.

Each day I thank God that I can eat, drink, get dressed, seek to do his will, *now*. For those things I am tempted to take for granted, I thank God. We've got meat; that's a blessing, that's a miracle. And then I pray the most powerful prayer: "Lord, close the doors I don't need to walk through today. Open the doors that I do. Steer me away from people I don't need to deal with today. Put people in my path that I do. And, Lord, don't let me waste time."

When I say don't waste time, I don't mean you can't rest in the Lord. When you're resting in him, it's not wasting time to talk to people who call you. The Holy Spirit will prompt you. You've already asked him. He says, "Okay, I'm here to comfort you, to guide you, to provide for you, to convict you. So I'm going to do that." It's not fearful; it's liberating. Not wasting time doesn't mean packing more things in. It means using our time wisely. It could be sitting down and talking to somebody for an hour or two. You might have spent time you thought you didn't have doing that, but when you come back to whatever you were doing, the Lord will give you the knowledge to get everything done or the wisdom to know you didn't have to do it today.

Of course, there's not a week that passes that I don't need the Lord's admonition to be anxious for nothing. But he will work everything out. He has ordered this day. Let us rejoice in it as a gift from him.

*This day, Lord, I accept this day as a gift from you. I want to spend my time according to your wisdom and guidance. Make me sensitive to how you desire to order my day. Amen.*

# *Anger Is Not a Virtue!*

I will never forget that October night when I deplaned at Washington National Airport on my way to Indian Head, Maryland, for a speaking engagement. The weather was pleasant outside, but my thoughts were tossing and turning on the inside. I'd been informed earlier in the day that in Indian Head, everything shut down in the early evening. The motel closed at ten o'clock. Out of the sympathy of her heart, a woman was going to stay there until midnight. If I didn't get there before midnight, I wouldn't have a place to stay. I'd be on my own.

The five o'clock flight from Houston to Washington, D.C., was delayed more than two hours. We sat on the runway in Houston all that time — time enough for me to start a whirlwind in my head. *What if I get to Indian Head and the woman is gone? What if I don't get there at all tonight? I have to speak at eight o'clock in the morning! What if my commute to Indian Head takes longer than I expect? What if the car rental counter is closed when I get there? What are my options?*

While my mind imagined various catastrophes, I developed a plan. *When I get off the plane, I will have my driver's license and confirmation number readily available for the car rental clerk. He or she will have empathy for me and will get me out of there quickly and efficiently.* I had it all figured out — I thought!

I dashed off the plane and proceeded directly to the car rental counter, prepared with all the identification needed to make it a quick and easy transaction. My plan didn't work. The clerk had tunnel vision. I offered her my driver's license and confirmation number and asked her to enter them into the computer so the profile would give her instructions concerning the car. Her response to me was, "I need to see your credit card." I replied, "Yes, ma'am, I understand. However, if you will input my confirmation number, it will show you my profile, including my credit card information." She demanded, "I said, I need to see your credit card!" "Trust me," I answered, "if you will put the information into your computer, you will see what to do. This is an unusual situation, ma'am. I need to get to Indian Head, Maryland, before midnight." It was already 11:30 P.M. With an indignant tone of voice, the clerk exclaimed, "You must not have heard what I said. I said, *I need to see your credit card!*"

That did it! I lost my cool. I screeched, "Woman, you better put in my confirmation number if you know what's good for you! I'm going to Indian Head tonight if I have to take you with me." (I didn't realize until I left the counter that I was threatening to kidnap the woman.) I continued, "If you don't know what to do in unusual situations, ask somebody. Don't just tell me you need my credit card. If you would do what I ask, you would discover that the car rental is billed directly to the company I'm working for."

I continued my tirade until a young man came out of another area and asked what was going on. (He had heard me shouting, no doubt.) My gracious response to him was, "And who are *you*?" He told me he was the manager. Oh, boy, did I let him have it. I told him that he should be training people to understand and handle unusual situations, that as tired as travelers are at the end of a day, especially after waiting on a plane for more than two hours before takeoff, his clerks should be ready, willing, and able to give the most excellent customer service possible, which included listening to the customers!

He was so nice. He agreed with me. I had become so irate that I didn't even notice he'd taken my driver's license and confirmation number from me, put them into the computer, and presented me with car keys. He got my attention when he said the documents were in order, the car was ready, and he'd be happy to escort me to the vehicle.

Well, I wouldn't be outdone. With my hands on my hips and my eyebrows raised, I proclaimed angrily, "And anyway, do you know who I am? My name is Thelma Wells. I teach customer service all over the world." My eyes boring through the female clerk, I continued, "I teach people how *not* to get upset when they deal with people like *you.*" I was downright ugly.

When I eventually got to Indian Head (much past midnight), there was no room at the inn. The only place to stay in the small town was at that no-name motel. I'd have to bunk down in my car for the night. About 2:00 A.M., a woman came out of one of the rooms to get a soft drink. I asked her for a blanket because it was cold. She declined. I also asked her if there was anyplace for me to get some rest. She told me to go to the first signal light and make a right. I did. I drove and drove, endlessly, it seemed, down dark, winding roads. It was so dark I thought Big Foot would walk out of the forest any minute.

Just beyond a massive grove of trees I spotted a Shell service station sign. That was the most beautiful sign I had ever seen; it indicated that civilization was near. As I got to the intersection where the gas station was, I looked to my left and saw another beautiful sign: Motel 8. Swiftly I turned into the entrance, shuffled painfully to the office, and pounded on the door to get the desk clerk's attention. The woman was compassionate. Even though the motel was closed, she invited me in and comforted me while I told her about my ordeal. Thank God, I finally had a resting place if only for one hour. It seemed like the fastest hour in my sleep history.

Five A.M. came too soon. Time to arise and make that forty-five-minute trip from La Plata, Maryland, to Indian Head. I had to get back in time to stand in line with the construction workers and other contractors for a pass to enter the naval base where I was teaching.

Miraculously the day went well. Four o'clock came quickly, and I was off to Washington National Airport and the infamous car rental counter. I had more than an hour to think about the previous day and how I'd responded. I was not proud of myself. As a customer service and how-to-deal-with-difficult-people trainer, I had not done a good job of walking the talk. I had lost perspective on who I was and whose I was. I had allowed myself to act totally in the flesh.

When I'd asked the people at the car rental counter if they knew who I was, that question should have been directed to me. *Thelma, do you know who you are? Do you know who you are representing everywhere you go? Do you think Christ would have acted as you did? Do you think the Lord is proud of your conduct? Do you have a repentant heart for the way you acted? Thelma, as a Christian, what are you going to do when you get back to that car rental counter?*

I walked up to the counter. The woman who provoked me was standing with her back to me, facing the computer. I spoke to her. She looked around and saw me, then immediately turned back to face the computer. I spoke to her again in a pleading voice in an attempt to communicate, *I'm sorry for the way I acted.* Without turning to me, she shook her head. She would not let me apologize.

I've reflected on that situation for many years and have concluded that the clerk did not, in fact, "make" me mad. I responded to her based on the storm that was raging within me. I felt totally at the clerk's mercy. When I felt I had no control, I fell apart and made a spectacle of myself.

As Christians, how often do we operate in the flesh and allow our jumbled thoughts and emotions to dictate our conduct? When I rushed into Washington National, I had already set the stage for that unsettling interaction. The what-ifs had me, and I wasn't going to be taken alive! So I worried and schemed. I don't remember asking God to take charge of the situation and have his way with it. I don't remember asking for protection and grace. I don't remember asking him to give me peace in the middle of the storm.

The fact is, when we take charge of a situation without consulting the wisdom of God, we always make a mess of it. Relationships get convoluted, hearts get broken, unfair and unkind words are spoken, egos are crushed, waves of doubt trouble us, distrust creeps in, guilt takes up residence, and emotions go haywire. *Thangs ain't purty.*

Think of the times you become angry or out of control. What's happening? Do you feel safe and secure? Do you feel competent and confident? Do you have faith that God is in perfect control of your life? I don't think so.

What do you think would happen in our lives if we would maintain an attitude of prayer in every situation?

What might have happened had I not attempted to manipulate the situation at the car rental desk? I believe I would have left there in time to make it to Indian Head before midnight. I know I would not have been hostile and belligerent. I would have been able to walk back up to that rental desk with a clear conscience. I certainly would have had more of a mind to thank God for his favor and protection on the trip.

Thank God, he never gives up on remaking us in his image! No matter how obnoxious our behavior is at times, he is willing to convict and correct us so that we can become more like him.

*Lord, thank you for giving me all the ammunition I need to hold back the enemy called anger. Too often I take that innate emotion and use it against your will to accomplish my own will. How often I stumble and make a mess! I take charge, talk out of turn, and refuse to listen to you as I should. Too often I already have my mind made up about how things should be. Your Word says that you are gracious and full of compassion, slow to anger, and of great mercy. By the power of the Holy Spirit, please conform me to your image. Amen.*

# Did I Have to Get Burned to Listen?

We'd had a wonderful Fourth of July. Our children, their spouses, our grandchildren, and other relatives gathered at our home to eat fried shrimp, mashed potatoes, catfish, hush puppies, potato salad, lemonade, and ice cream. It was good (if I have to say so myself!).

After everyone had left, I had a serious craving for more shrimp. So I fixed some for George and me. We ate and reminisced about the day's activities. It had been a perfect day—talking, laughing, and enjoying our family. Now that I was alone with my honey, I rose to clean the kitchen. Then I could spend the rest of the evening with him.

The grease from the deep fryer was still hot. Because I didn't want to wait until it cooled, I lifted the deep fryer and started to pour the grease into a plastic storage container. Well, you can imagine what happened next. The plastic container started to melt, and I impulsively dropped the deep fryer. Hot grease splashed all over my right arm and hand.

*Oh! Mercy! I'm on fire! Don't panic! Get ice water! Get the medical book! Call 911! Do something!* My mind was in a whirlwind. My husband rushed me to the emergency room. After being treated, I learned that I had second- and third-degree burns.

I was not instructed to rest. And even if I had been, I probably would not have. I had too much to do. Yes, the pain was excruciating, but I had to speak at a conference the following day. And for months I had planned a trip with my daughter and grandson to the National Speakers Association annual convention the following week. I was scheduled to sing with an ensemble at the convention and participate on a panel. I had to be there. I had given my word.

By the time I arrived at the convention, I was exhausted. I was too tired to move. I tried to get out of bed but couldn't. My head was spinning, arm hurting, stomach rolling, body aching. I was sick! My immune system had shut down. I forced myself to keep my obligations (foolish, I know) because I wanted to keep my word. I figured that's what God would want (but did I really ask him?).

I became more ill. The doctor at a local clinic informed me that I had a 104-degree temperature and gastritis. "Go home," he said. "Take these antibiotics. Drink plenty of water. Get some rest!" I finally did. I had no other choice.

Three days later at 3:19 in the morning, God woke me up. I sat up in bed just listening. I couldn't do much more. In the stillness I heard from God. In my spirit I knew he was telling me that my life was taking a new direction. Certain paths had come to an end and other paths were emerging. Finally he had my undivided attention. It had been too long since I had *really* stopped to ask him what he would have me do. I'd been too busy forging my own agenda. Perhaps if I had not become sick and bedridden, I would not have sat still long enough to hear God speak to me so effectively. I'm sure he wanted to communicate with me earlier—on less painful terms—but I was just too harried.

You don't have to learn the hard way as I did. You don't have to get burned to slow down and listen. You can stop and listen to God every day, quiet your spirit before him, ask him to communicate with you. God has plenty to say to you, but he requires your undivided attention. Psalm 46:10 tells us that we will *know* God and his sovereignty when we are "still." Be still and know his will for you today.

*Father, you know all I have promised to do. What with home, church, social activities, and other responsibilities, I barely have time to breathe. Help me to slow down. Help me to just say no sometimes. I know you desire and deserve my time and my quiet dependence on your guidance. I want to hear from you. Remind me to stop, listen, and wait on you each day. Amen.*

# I Thought I Knew What I Was Doing

I don't like going to meetings. I found little value in attending the meetings of the organizations I used to affiliate with. So when Dennis McCuistion invited me to become a member of the North Texas Speakers Association (NTSA), I wasn't interested. He kept telling me that I was missing a great opportunity to improve my speaking business, but I was already a *successful* speaker so what could NTSA offer me except a time commitment I didn't want?

Dennis and I met in the late 1970s when we were both teaching for the Dallas chapter of the American Institute of Banking, and we got better acquainted when we became members of the board of directors of the same banking organization. Since that time, Dennis and I had become professional speakers. Dennis had gotten involved in the North Texas Speakers Association and the National Speakers Association (NSA) and realized the value of these organizations. Because my business was thriving, I really thought I knew everything there was to know about what I was doing.

Each time Dennis called to invite me to an NTSA meeting, I had an excuse to decline. But Dennis was his usual persistent self and wouldn't take no for an answer. Finally I agreed to attend one meeting to get him off my back.

That Saturday morning in 1986 was truly an eye-opening, humbling experience. I learned more about the business of speaking that morning than I could have learned in five years of owning the business. I became keenly aware of the fact that professional speaking was actually a business for me, no longer just a hobby. If I was to continue to succeed in this business, I'd better get organized, keep up-to-date documentation, and do a more professional job of contracting with my customers. I thought I was doing things very well. *Not!*

One other important fact stood out to me: The people in the organization were willing and happy to give one another information and guide one another in the right direction. I didn't know anyone but Dennis, yet they were willing to share information with me that could help me be a better professional. *Wow! What a giving group!* I thought. *I think I'm liking this.*

They announced that the National Speakers Association was sponsoring an upcoming workshop in San Antonio. I decided then and there to attend. The local chapter seemed too good to be true; perhaps the real scoop about this national organization would be revealed at the San Antonio meeting. When I went, I discovered the truth. The organization was indeed caring and giving. The workshops were full of information that I could use immediately. I was convinced: This was the organization for me!

In June I received a telephone call from the NSA informing me that I had been selected to present a showcase (an eight-minute keynote) at the NSA convention in Phoenix the following month. Me? Speak for the National Speakers Association? The caller assured me that she had the right person. Dennis' wife, Nikki, had sent my brochure and audiotape to the NSA without my knowledge. There was one little hitch: Speakers are required to be members of the NSA, and I was not. "Ma'am, how much is the membership fee?" I asked the caller. She told me, and I promptly wrote the check and sent it by overnight mail. I would speak in front of the NSA in July.

The knowledge I gained from this group tremendously enhanced my professional speaking career. The day I presented my showcase, one of the owners of CareerTrack was in the audience. Within one month, I was traveling and teaching for CareerTrack, a national seminar company that contracts professional speakers to teach business courses throughout the world. That period of time in my career propelled me to a more prominent position in the professional speaking arena. My visibility increased in industries I had not previously penetrated, and I gained credibility because of my association with professional speaking organizations. The peak of my NSA activities was when I was asked to deliver a keynote address in a general session at the Dallas national convention. It was the first time in the history of the NSA that a black woman was center stage before the entire convention. I would have missed the eventful occasion if I had not listened to Dennis and attended an NTSA meeting. I have learned to never say never. As determined as I was not to join another organization that meets regularly, by getting involved I estimate that I cut my learning curve for running my business by about five years.

God uses many methods to prepare us for the tasks he has assigned. Increasing our knowledge is not confined to the Bible; it is also confirmed by the Bible. Being open to learning from different sources is a sign of wisdom.

*God, I don't know everything about anything. Thank you for both the obvious and the unexpected opportunities you give me to increase my knowledge so that I can serve you better. Help me to seek after knowledge as I seek after wisdom. Amen.*

# God Sent Us to College

When I was a girl, my family was poor and had no means of saving money for my college education. Granny, Daddy Lawrence, and Uncle Jim made sure I had the necessities and some of the luxuries of life so I didn't know we were poor or just how poor we were until I got old enough to read the poverty indexes.

Oh, how I wanted to go to college! After the secretarial school I tried to enroll in threw me out because of the color of my skin, Granny and I became more and more determined to find a way for me to go to college. Granny talked to her employer, Mrs. Mary Less, who was a wealthy white woman living in University Park in Dallas. Granny was one of her maids. Mrs. Less asked me to come to her house to discuss my college aspirations. When I did, she offered to send me to North Texas State University. She would pay my tuition and buy my books on the condition that I kept my grades above a C. If I got married before graduation, my husband would have to cover my bills.

Was I excited or what? Mrs. Less kept her end of the bargain. Daddy Lawrence gave me five dollars a month for the Laundromat, and Granny sent me "care packages." My roommates and I cooked at our off-campus home, and we walked to school so there was no need of transportation money. God *did* make a way.

When my husband and I got married on April 1, 1961, Mrs. Less's obligation became null and void. Thank God, my husband realized what he was going to have to do to send me to college. He did. I graduated from North Texas State University in August 1963 after getting married, changing my major from business administration to secondary education, having one child, and conceiving my second one.

My daughter Vikki wanted to attend the University of Texas at Austin. When she applied, our income was high, but so was our debt. I went to Austin during student orientation and waited for almost an entire week to meet with the financial counselor assigned to Vikki. Once I had a chance to talk with her, she told me that Vikki's loan had been approved for $269. *Say what? Two hundred sixty-nine dollars for four years? I don't think so!* I showed her our income statement and all the bills we owed. I needed to prove to her that even though we made money, we were living from one paycheck to the next. (That's nothing to be proud of, but in 1979 I didn't have the same money management skills I have now.)

Miss Smothers tried to prove to me via computer that Vikki's financial aid application had already been processed and that there was nothing else that could be done about the results. But after she'd spent about twenty minutes attempting to pull up Vikki's record on the screen with no success, I had her attention. Miss Smothers consented to reenter our financial statistics, and when she ran the new data through the computer, she was able to match Vikki up with more academic scholarships and work-study than my daughter needed for the entire four years! God knew what he had in store for Vikki's future and saw to it that she got her education, regardless of the financial limitations of her parents. God sent Vikki to college.

My younger daughter, Lesa, never wanted to go to a four-year college. Her goal was to become a hairstylist and own her own business. To be a successful businessperson, she decided she needed to take business courses at Mountain View Community College in Dallas. By the time Lesa was ready to start community college, we were financially prepared to send her. (She is seven years younger than Vikki.) However, we didn't have to pay for Lesa's education, either. The Branch/Roland Scholarship Committee at St. John's Missionary Baptist Church gave her a scholarship to Mountain View, and Mrs. Ella Mae Rollins paid for her beauty school education. Now Lesa is the owner of her own beauty salon where six operators help people look beautiful every week. Praise God!

Little George had the good fortune of working in a jewelry store when he was in high school. The master jeweler in that store took George under his wing and taught him all he knew about jewelry repair and design. George also attended the Gemological Institute of America to hone his skills. He now works for one of the largest jewelry companies in America.

You may have some dreams and goals that seem unreachable. Sometimes we can't see how we can possibly accomplish our objectives. But I'm here to tell you that if you keep the faith and trust in the Lord, he will open doors that you have no idea exist. What Granny said is true: Whatever you want bad enough that's within the perfect will of God, the Lord will make a way for it to come to pass. You better believe it!

*Lord God, you are awesome! You are the God of computers, education, money, and all good things that come our way. Thank you for making a way when it seems there is no way. Thank you for placing people in my life who care about my future and are willing to be used by you to accomplish your will for my life. You are truly an omnipotent God! Help me to hold on to the truth that you have everything under your control; you will work it out. Amen.*

## My Child Would Never Do That!

One of the most devastating truths for parents, especially Christian parents, is that their children can and do stray from their teachings. Many kids get involved in drugs, sex, pornography, witchcraft, or gangs; become school dropouts; abuse their parents; defy authority; and behave in many other heartbreaking ways.

I remember, during the early days of my teaching career, going to a friend's house to inform her that her son was breaking into the vending machines at school. She was furious with me. "My child would never do that!" she told me emphatically. "We give him everything he needs. You'd better stop lying about him." I took her cue and stopped telling her anything about her child, but I continued to watch the situation. While his mother remained in her denial, the child got more and more into a life of crime. To this day he's in trouble with the law.

There came a time in my life when shocking information was presented to me concerning children I had tried to influence. I discovered that they were experimenting with drugs. At first I blamed their peers. Then I pointed the finger back at the parents and eventually at God. After all, didn't his Word say, "Train a child in the way he should go, and when he is old he will not turn from it" (Prov. 22:6)? That's a principle that many

Christians refer to without fully understanding its meaning. What was God doing?

As I pondered the meaning of this Scripture, I wondered if I was missing something. I studied the word *train* and discovered it means "to dedicate." Parents must commit themselves to training their children in the ways of God. We must attempt to create in our children a desire and appetite to experience God for themselves. We must dedicate our children to God and dedicate ourselves to the stewardship of our children that God has entrusted us with. But we must remember that the world, with its evil charm and cunning influence, is used to persuading children to sin. Choices are offered; wrong choices often are made. Paul wrote, "For all have sinned and fall short of the glory of God" (Rom. 3:23 NKJV).

So what's the deal? I went back and read the proverb carefully. I realized it didn't promise that our children would *never* stray from the path we set them on; it said, "When he is *old* he will not turn from it." As the years have gone by, I've seen that principle fulfilled. For a long time, Satan confused these children's minds and bodies, but not their souls. Even while they strayed, they never forgot their parents' biblical teachings. Scripture still rang in their ears. Respect for Jesus remained deeply embedded in their hearts. I watched a long progression of some of these children from hostile, headstrong, immature kids to determined, funny, happy, God-loving adults.

God's Word is true. And when we feed it to our children, it will not return to him void. Isaiah 55:11 declares,

> So is my word that goes out from my mouth:
> It will not return to me empty,
> but will accomplish what I desire
> and achieve the purpose for which I sent it.

Our God has promised never to leave us or forsake us (Deut. 31:8). Children do stray. But God doesn't abandon them. We may hold fast to his promise to remain faithful to them.

*Lord, sometimes I get frustrated and frightened when you let children continue in their temptations and sins. I need strength to continue praying that they will not permanently depart from the teaching that has been instilled in them. Thank you for the encouragement that you will never leave them or forsake them. Help me as a parent to train my children in your ways, and then give me the faith to trust you to bring the work you've begun in them to completion. Amen.*

# Why Do You Complain?

Elle was one of the most reliable, conscientious, hard-working people in my bookkeeping department at the bank. She was always on time, didn't take advantage of breaks, took little or no sick leave. She was a loyal employee. There was only one big thing wrong: she whined, complained, and behaved like a victim all the time. There was not a day that she didn't come to my office to tell me what some other employee was or was not doing. She felt she was the only person working and carrying the load in the department. Everyone else was talking on the telephone, going to the rest room too much, chatting with other employees, coming back late from lunch, or doing something she considered worth reporting. I wondered how she could do all the work she was doing and keep tabs on everybody else. She made such a habit of coming into my office to complain that every time I saw her coming, my nose started to itch. I was not comfortable with the state of affairs!

When I became a supervisor, I had absolutely no supervisory training. I didn't have an educated clue about what I was supposed to do about an employee like Elle. I just had to rely on common sense. One weekend, after being perplexed all week about what I needed to do to stop her complaints, I came up with a brilliant idea. I created a form that listed every employee's name, and I left space for Elle to enter information about what the other people in the department were doing. I would make Elle the monitor of the bookkeeping department. Job description: Snoop on everybody and write it down. Report back to me with documentation of everyone's behavior.

Monday came and Elle didn't disappoint me. When she came into my office, I was ready for her. I was actually excited to see her. I asked her to be seated and told her how happy I was that she had taken it upon herself to look out for the department's well-being. I showed her the form I had created with all her colleagues' names and specific columns to record the various behaviors that she was to monitor. I told her, "Elle, I'm making you the official watcher of the department. These people are not pulling their load, and we need to nip this in the bud. I want you to document what they're doing. If they go to the rest room and stay too long, write it down. If you think they're on a personal phone call, write it down. If you see them clocking in on more than one time card, write it down. If they go to lunch early or return late, write that down. If they talk ugly to the customers, write that down. I want you to record every wrong thing they do and report back to me in one month. When you bring the documentation to me, bring the people with you too. We'll stop this!"

Elle was horrified. She responded with an emphatic no. She did not want to cause a problem; she just thought I wanted to know what was going on in the department. She could not bring "those people" into my office. She wasn't that brave! Her refusal didn't surprise me at all. She didn't want to confront her colleagues face-to-face. She wanted to come in and complain to me. I told Elle that if she could not comply with what I asked, she should never come in again complaining and whining without documentation and the person in tow.

I nipped that thing in the bud, all right. Elle never whined to me again. But the situation still perplexed me.

I wondered why Elle thought it was so important to tattle on other people. I knew she was much older than some of her other colleagues and she had been on the job for many years. She had no academic skills, just the skills she had developed on the job. She was her sole support. She was a loner and lived a lonely life, with only her cat to keep her company. Her son and daughter visited sometimes, but she didn't seem to have much of a social life. I was concerned about her.

Later I was promoted to supervisor of the personal banking division of the bank. Having worked first as a new accounts clerk and then as a bookkeeping supervisor, I had learned a lot about the needs of both areas. One of the most poorly managed areas in the bank was the signature cards and other account documents. Those documents were used by several departments, but no one was in charge of holding people accountable for taking them out of the files and returning them. More often than not, someone would come to look for a file, and nobody would know where it was. The situation needed attention. And I had the perfect solution!

I made Elle the official guardian of the signature cards and resolution files. She was free to rearrange the files in a more functional way so that she could get to them easily. She developed a form like a library rental card to check the documents in and out to employees. On the form were the name and department of the person, the time of day, the due date, and any other information Elle thought pertinent.

I have never seen anyone perk up and look as needed and important as Elle did. What she'd really wanted all along was to be assured that her job was secure. I discovered that all her whining and complaining was a smoke screen for what was really happening inside. Elle was scared of being replaced by someone who was younger or had more education. By creating that job for Elle, I gave her what she needed. She was able to regain her confidence and be proud of the job she was doing without the interference of all "those other people." When it was time for Elle to retire, she did so with dignity and security.

Sometimes people we think are chronic whiners, complainers, or victims may be sending us a message. They may be trying to tell us that they're afraid and need assurance and support. The experience with Elle has helped me be less critical of people who exhibit similar behavior. I have learned that there is a reason people act the way they do.

Just as Elle was acting out of fear, so do many Christians. Experts believe that most people have four basic fears:

The fear of failure.
The fear of rejection.
The fear of risk or loss.
The fear of success.

I'm sure everybody has had all these fears at one time or another. That's only human. However, the Bible has something to say about how Christians should respond to fear: "The fear of man bringeth a snare: but whoso putteth his trust in the LORD shall be safe" (Prov. 29:25 KJV). Fear can be a reliable deterrent to an unsafe or harmful situation, or it can paralyze our efforts to move from one place to another in our lives.

By admitting to the fear and allowing myself to analyze *why* I'm afraid, I usually discover I don't know how to do something or how it will turn out if I do. It's good for me to talk about it to another Christian who I know will offer me godly counsel. The Bible is full of passages that console me and give me strength as I walk through that period of fear. And then, either I tackle the situation with all the ammunition possible, or I delegate it to some-one with more expertise. I try to remember that when I am obedient to God and work to satisfy his will, I can claim Isaiah 54:4: "Fear not; for thou shalt not be ashamed: neither be thou confounded" (KJV). Elle was not shamed. Through concern and observation, using com-mon sense, I was able to understand her situation and do something about it.

Whatever your fear, God has someone or something in place to help you. Whining, complaining, and behav-ing like a victim are not viable ways to resolve your fears. Such behavior only makes them worse because each time you talk about your fears without resolving them, you are rehearsing them instead of dispelling them. Problems become more and more intense and ingrained as you constantly discuss them.

You can change your behavior. Think about the things that cause you the most fear. Ask yourself why you're so afraid. Talk about the fear to someone you trust. Pray to God to help you overcome it. Study what the Bible says about fear. Sing praises to God or listen to music that gives praise to God. Willingly release the fear. Watch God work in your life to replace fear with confidence!

*Father, I am so glad I can call you Father because good fathers listen to their children's fears and do something to help them overcome them. There are so many places in the Bible where you tell us not to fear, for you are our refuge. You take good pleasure in pro-tecting us. How grateful I am that when I am afraid, you never shame me, but you deliver me and set my feet upon a rock. Amen.*

# Who Likes Criticism?

I don't know anyone who really enjoys being criticized. But whether we like it or not, criticism is what all of us get at one time or another. Sometimes constructive criticism is easier to take than ruthless faultfinding, but criticism is criticism. It's rarely pleasant.

One day I was preparing to go into a seminar when a woman I didn't know walked up to me and said, "Your hair sure is an ugly color." (Admittedly I kept cosmetic companies in business because at that time I colored my hair every six weeks. That particular week my hair was Sparkling Sherry.)

I responded to this lovely woman this way: "Thank you. I'm glad you were paying attention to my hair. I color it every six weeks. The next time I do, I'll remember what you said. It's always great to have an unbiased opinion."

She was speechless. I had taken her power away! Perhaps she thought she could make me feel bad, but she was wrong. The fact is, I had looked in the mirror that morning and left home pleased with the way I looked (hair included). I had a choice when she said those critical words to me. I could have responded with hostility and anger. I could have ignored her. I could have used my sense of humor. I chose the latter. I turned a potentially negative statement into a positive response.

Some of the best growing I've ever done has been the result of criticism, whether constructive or destructive. In my opinion, constructive criticism occurs when someone addresses the situation instead of the person, for example: "Betty, I have some questions about this report because it doesn't seem to be complete. Can you tell me what to look for or how it can be corrected?" Destructive criticism tears down the person instead of addressing the situation appropriately. "Betty, you made a mistake on this report. Can't you ever complete a task? Get this corrected and give it back to me."

One of the most powerful people in my early corporate career was an officer at a bank where I worked. She could correct me and criticize me, yet make me happy. I remember several times I goofed up an account. She would come quietly to my desk and ask to speak to me in private. Her comments generally ran along these lines: "Thelma, you are learning this business quickly. I'm proud of your progress. We do have a situation that needs your attention. Mrs. Whoever called and said her checks were ordered incorrectly. I see that your name is on the order. Can you please find out what happened, who was affected by what happened, and how we can prevent this from happening again? You can get back to me before leaving today if you get this information. Thank you. I know you'll take care of it for us."

Man, did I feel important! I thought, *She trusts me to get this information to her. Boy, I'm good.* As I would go through the process of getting the information, I would learn more and more about ways each department depended on the others, how to be more observant, and so forth. The officer was teaching me all the time she was criticizing me.

Even when we don't enjoy being criticized, we must admit we learn some things about ourselves that we'd have never known had we not been criticized. Over the years, I've learned techniques for taking the sting out of receiving criticism so I can benefit from it. This is what helps me:

- I consider the source. Is the person criticizing me genuinely interested in my well-being?
- I consider the circumstances. Am I clear on the circumstances that caused the criticism?
- If the criticism is appropriate and accurate, I agree with it. Who is going to argue with me when I'm agreeing with her?
- If I wish to have more explanation concerning the situation, I ask for it. Getting complete information about why someone said something or what's wrong with something is another way to learn.
- If I don't agree but don't want to have a damaged relationship, I evade the issue by using noncommittal words such as *maybe, I guess, it seems, possibly, you think? Perhaps, I'll try,* and phrases that don't cost me anything but make the person feel that I'm agreeing with him.

Maybe one reason I've been married as long as I have is that I use that last technique with my husband! Sometimes when he's fussing at me about something, I say, "Honey, perhaps you're right. Maybe I need to listen to you more. The next time this happens, I'll try to pay more attention. Thank you for calling this to my attention." I don't admit to anything, but what I say sure makes him feel good.

On the other hand, criticism can be very wise counsel when accepted with an open mind. The book of Proverbs talks a lot about it. Read Proverbs 8:14; 12:15; 15:22; 19:20; 20:5; and 27:9. Remember, when you're faced with criticism, you have a choice. You can get hostile and defensive, or you can heed King Solomon's words and follow his advice. Basically he was saying, "A wise person takes criticism and extracts from it what can help her to grow. A foolish person denounces criticism and stunts her growth."

Be wise. Grow from criticism.

*Lord, you use some unique methods to help me become what you want me to be. Criticism does not make me feel good; who wants to hear what's wrong about him or her? But wise counsel is so important to you that the wisest man who ever lived took a lot of time to write about it, under your direction. Frankly, God, I can always use feedback to help me become a more excellent servant for you. Help me to take it in the right spirit and to use it wisely. Amen.*

## Victims or Victors?

One of the hardest demands God makes of his children is the one that calls us to love our enemies—to forgive people who have knowingly and willfully violated us physically, emotionally, or spiritually. When we are hurt by the infidelity of a spouse, abuse from a loved one, vicious gossip, unfair treatment at work, crime, or humiliation, the wound goes deep. Anything that threatens our security, safety, integrity, intelligence, or character is difficult to cope with, much less to forgive.

At one time in my life, I really hated some people who had hurt me. God knew that sometimes I wanted to see them dead. I obsessed about their deeds and daydreamed about what I would do to get even. Yes, I did! Here I was, thinking I was a good Christian woman with tons of hatred and vengeance, wrath and hostility, in my heart. I believe my unforgiving spirit eventually manifested itself in a two-and-a-half-year bout with a physical ailment called phlebitis. Having pain and redness in my left leg and wearing heavy elastic stockings to aid blood circulation were part of my daily routine. Medicines my doctors prescribed weren't helping. Not even the painful injections I got in my stomach to aid blood coagulation were helping. I was in the hospital several times, and I missed a lot of work. Whenever I sat down, I had to elevate my legs to keep a blood clot from forming and possibly killing me. I was a mess!

Thank God for true friends. Orniece Shelby came to see me and offered a different prescription altogether. "Thelma," she said, "I really believe you'll get well if you forgive the people who have hurt you. Whatever it is, let it go!" To that insulting statement, I made an emphatic, uncharacteristically harsh reply, telling her where she could go for saying something like that to me. (I was not as strong in my Christian walk then as I am now.)

Several weeks passed, and I wasn't getting better. Orniece came to see me again and told me the same thing. "Thelma, baby, I believe you'd get well if you would just forgive them for what they did to you." That time I wasn't quite so defensive. My friend had planted a seed of truth, and the Holy Spirit had begun to water it.

By the third time Orniece urged me to forgive, I had become convinced that something might indeed be going on inside me, stifling the healing process. I decided to take my friend's prescription, which included reading my Bible and asking God to help me forgive. Notice, I was not to ask to be healed of phlebitis, but to be given a forgiving heart.

Over time I began to submit to God's will for me to forgive. I asked him to make it convenient for me to see the people I hated and to help me tell them, "I forgive you." One Thursday after my regular weekly laboratory visit during which the technician tested my blood for a medication adjustment, I stopped by an automobile parts store. Guess who was there? Yes, the two people I hated. I had asked God to make it convenient for me to tell them I forgave them. He did. (Watch what you pray for, you might get it sooner than you think!)

My heart was pumping overtime. My hands began to sweat. My tongue was heavy. I thought about the vow I made to God, and I remembered that it's better to never make a vow than to make one and break it (Eccl. 5:5). My moment of truth had arrived. With fear and trembling, I approached my enemies, told them I was keenly aware of the things that had happened and how hurt I had been, but I wanted them to know that I forgave them. They were shocked!

When I left their presence, I felt as if the weight of the world had been lifted off my shoulders. I was delighted by my ability to express genuine forgiveness to them after seriously wanting something bad to happen to them. At that moment, I became a victor instead of a victim. God restored the joy of my salvation. I was given back my song of praise. Boy, did I feel different!

When I returned home the following Thursday from my weekly laboratory visit, my doctor called me to report how pleased he was with my progress. He said the tests showed that I had begun to respond favorably to the medication. Tremendous progress continued for the next few weeks until I decided, *No more medicine.* I knew deep in my heart that I was delivered from my grudges and hatred, and I was healed of my dreaded condition. Praise the name of Jesus!

Now, please don't misunderstand me. I am not saying that all people who are sick are in that condition because they harbor resentments. But I am saying that hatred and lack of forgiveness will manifest themselves in one way or another. Trying to get even with people who have hurt us drains our energy and diminishes our productivity. Holding on to our hurts will always have a negative effect on our lives.

Sometimes we just don't want to let go of our grudges and heartaches. We want to hold on to them and watch our enemies suffer. We look for opportunities to bring up the past and rub the guilty persons' faces in what they've done. But while we're in the "get back at them" stage, we are constantly rehashing their actions toward us, our reactions toward them, and our hopes for their destruction. Resentment spreads like a cancer, eating away at the soul. It destroys our hopes and relationships. I know. I've been there.

Have you been there? Are you there now? Maybe your lack of forgiveness has caused guilt feelings, oversensitivity, physical ailments, poor relationships, problems on the job, lack of trust of others, paralyzing fear of the unknown, or something else that hinders your experience of the abundant life Christ promises. If this is true, you can ask God to help you become willing to forgive, and ultimately to speak forgiveness to those who have hurt you.

Jesus told us that if we are unwilling to forgive, we will not be forgiven. Friend, don't miss out on God's precious grace. Allow the Holy Spirit to administer the healing medicine of forgiveness.

*Father, how deeply I appreciate that you are willing to forgive me for every wrong I've ever done. For you, it is a joy to forgive. The beautiful thing about your forgiveness is that you never rub my nose in my past transgressions. You choose to "remember my sin no more." Please grant me a forgiving heart like yours. Help me to let go of my grudges and the bitterness of my past so that I can be a victor instead of a victim. The power to forgive is such sweetness in my soul. Amen.*

# *Praise Is a Two-Way Street*

I've always enjoyed praising God in song. Singing praise and worship songs has calmed me when I'm upset, adjusted my attitude when it gets out of whack, given me patience when I'm restless, and infused me with the sheer pleasure of making music to the Lord. I love to sing!

For years, the idea of producing a music album was tucked back in the recesses of my mind. I thought about it now and then, but I assumed that the probability was remote. My children and several friends had suggested I produce an album, but frankly I didn't think my voice was recording quality. I sang in church sometimes, and I was always singing at home. Sometimes I sang at the end of my speaking engagements and occasionally at weddings. That was certainly no reason to get my hopes up about being a recording artist.

One evening in August 1996, I was driving south on Interstate 35 in Dallas, and the thought came to me again to cut a music album. *Now, what is this, Lord? I can't do that! Besides, I'm in the middle of preparing for my annual Becoming a Woman of Excellence retreat. I don't have time to deal with a music album.* (Sometimes I argue with God.) I put the thought out of my mind and continued with my plans for the upcoming retreat.

A month later the retreat was behind me, and the idea about recording an album jumped into my mind again as

I was driving to work one morning. That time the voice within got more specific. The Holy Spirit seemed to direct me: *Cut the album the weekend before Thanksgiving.* God had my attention. *All right, all right! Whatever you say, Sir!* (I ought to know by now that I'll never win when I try to argue with God.) I called my daughter Vikki, and we started planning immediately.

We began to put the pieces together for what we called a Thanksgiving Gala, to be held at St. John Missionary Baptist Church on November 23, 1996. Vikki made all the arrangements with the recording company, worked out stage and set decorations and lighting, music permissions and contracts, musicians and soloists. My office staff busily prepared invitations, news releases, publicity, and every other detail to make the recorded worship program a success, honoring the Lord. My role in the entire project was minimal. I would simply sing, along with other "unknowns" whom we believed had anointed voices and would allow their talents to be used for the glory of God.

The night of the Gala arrived. The audience attendance was good. The stage and the lighting were warm and worshipful. The recording company was skilled and professional. The music was outstanding! People are still talking about the sacredness and quality of the program. The audiocassette, *Jesus, We Give Thanks,* is comforting people in hospitals and nursing homes, and blessing people in their homes, offices, and cars all over the nation. People are calling and faxing in orders for more and more tapes. Some people have ordered twenty at a time!

I cringe when I think what a major ministry opportunity I would have missed had I continued to ignore the Lord's prompting to produce an album. God had a definite plan in mind: He wanted me to help his people praise him. He has put the desire to worship deep within our hearts, and he wants us to raise our hearts and voices to him. The word *praise* is recorded in the Bible 216 times (according to *Strong's Concordance of the Bible*); it must be pretty important! Psalm 22:3 says that God inhabits our praise. When we worship, he is in our midst. That's why there is such great pleasure in honoring God with our praise for all he is and does, for his great love for humankind.

In Zephaniah 3, the prophet painted a magnificent picture of this holy love. After God condemned the religious people of the land for their moral decay, his merciful nature shone forth. He promised to gather his true children, the ones who offered him praise, and sustain them as he destroyed his enemies. He would restore their fortunes before their very eyes and give them back their joy. And God would respond to his people's praise with his own.

> The LORD your God is with you,
> he is mighty to save.
> He will take great delight in you,
> he will quiet you with his love,
> he will rejoice over you with singing.
>
> ZEPHANIAH 3:17

How awesome to know that the almighty God rejoices over us when we praise him!

Consider Psalm 147:1:

> Praise the LORD.
> How good it is to sing praises to our God,
> how pleasant and fitting to praise him!

It is *good* and *pleasant* to praise the Lord: good for him, pleasant for us. Praise is a two-way street. Hallelujah!

*Jesus, we give you thanks. Thank you for being an awesome God who deserves all our praise. You are the Holy One. You are the Precious One. You are the Alpha and Omega, the Master of everything. I love you, Lord. I hold you in highest esteem. How thrilling it is to hear you sing back to me when I lift my voice to you in praise! Amen.*

## His Eye Is on the Sparrow

My daughter Vikki was independent, adventurous, and courageous as a twenty-something young lady, and she had always wanted to see the world. She set out on an eighteen-country tour, and the first six months of her voyage from Dallas to Europe, Asia, and India went well. The next stop was to be Egypt, but God intervened.

She called me from an airport in India and said, "I'm not going on to Egypt as I'd planned. Something's telling me I need to leave and go to Germany. I'll call you in a few days when I get there."

Little did she know that the day after her departure, the day she was scheduled to be in Egypt, war broke out. Operation Desert Storm had begun. Had she gone to Egypt or remained in that area of the world, the possibility of her getting trapped there by the military is frightening to think about. Many Americans were caught there and were not permitted to leave for a number of days.

My son, George, lived in California for a short time. He was not accustomed to or familiar with gang activity. His knowledge of the gangs was limited to what he'd seen on television. But he learned quickly after living in the Los Angeles area for about a week.

One day he wore the wrong color shirt. George, an unsuspecting, happy-go-lucky young man, was leisurely walking to his friend Daryl's house. Daryl was watching out his window and realized the danger George was in.

Daryl yelled to George to hurry and get in the house before he was seen. Praise God, George listened. Just as he ran into the house, a carful of gang members drove by the house making loud, frightening threats.

George had another "scared stiff" experience while in California. He'd finished working at Sears that day, and on his way home he noticed a man who looked safe for him to speak to. Remember, George is from Texas. We speak to people whether we know them or not. George greeted the man with his usual friendliness, expecting a nod or verbal greeting in response. George got more than he bargained for. The man pulled out a gun, used profane invectives, said he was waiting for someone to kill that day, and George was the one.

Some people happened to be coming toward them, and George had gotten enough distance between him and the gunman to start running toward the people for protection. The crazy gunman turned away from George and went in the opposite direction. Whatever the gunman's rationale for not following through on his murderous urge, I believe God showed up again and spared George's life one more time.

In every situation, whether ordinary or life threatening, God assures us that he keeps his eye on us and knows the number of hairs on our heads. Absolutely everything that can happen to us—good, bad, or indifferent—God knows and cares about. God is concerned about us all the time, in every area of our lives, even if nobody else is. He promises that we are never away from his presence.

Does that mean nothing bad will ever happen to us? No. But it does mean that we can have inner peace in this dangerous world. Jesus declared, "I have told you these things, so that in me you may have peace. In this world you will have trouble. But take heart! I have overcome the world" (John 16:33).

God has promised to watch over his dominion children. Every trial, tribulation, question mark, perplexity, decision, burden, disappointment, heartache, calamity, tragedy, turmoil, loss, danger, exclusion, accusation, threat, or act of the Devil is within the scope of God's knowledge and care. He is sovereign, and he knows the outcome of whatever befalls us. He has already worked it out. His ministering angels protect us. His precious blood covers us. His grace and mercy go before us. He has told us,

> When you pass through the waters,
> I will be with you;
> and when you pass through the rivers,
> they will not sweep over you.
> When you walk through the fire,
> you will not be burned;
> the flames will not set you ablaze.
> For I am the LORD, your God,
> the Holy One of Israel, your Savior.
>
> ISAIAH 43:2–3

With that kind of assurance, I can sing the words of this hymn with confidence and faith:

> I trust in God wherever I may be,
> Upon the land or on the rolling sea,
> For, come what may,
> From day to day,
> My heav'nly Father watches over me.
> I trust in God, I know he cares for me
> On mountain bleak or on the stormy sea;
> Tho' billows roll,
> He keeps my soul.
> My heav'nly Father watches over me.*

---

*"My Heavenly Father Watches Over Me," by Charles H. Gabriel, Copyright 1910, renewed 1938. The Rodeheaver Co., owner.

*How consoling it is, Lord, to know without a doubt that everywhere I go, you are there watching over me. Thank you that you are omniscient, omnipresent, and omnipotent. Thank you that you are not limited by time, space, gravity, or atmosphere. Thank you that you prove your nearness in my most scary experiences. And thank you that no matter what I encounter in this world, you have already overcome it. Amen.*

## *Our God Reigns!*

The daughter of one of my good friends called me recently and asked me to speak for an annual religious conference. She was Muslim. I reminded her that I am a Christian. She replied that she knew I was a Christian, but her mother and sister-in-law had told her I was an excellent speaker and that they (the women of Islam) should ask me to speak at their women's conference. I explained to her that Jesus Christ is Lord of my life, and that I talk about Jesus in my speeches. She said, "Oh, just talk about male-female relationships and how you stayed married all these years. We want a mature lady who can be a role model for us in our marriages."

I hesitated before saying yes. As I thought about it, I was reminded of an occasional prayer of mine: "Lord, please give me opportunities to witness for you." And then I was reminded of what he'd told me to do as I was lying on the floor talking to him in 1995. I'd gotten the impression that he wanted me to accept every speaking invitation as an opportunity to proclaim a word for him. Jesus told his disciples, "The harvest is plentiful but the workers are few" (Matt. 9:37). Was I willing to work to gather the harvest? In my spirit, God reminded me that he would be with me. He goes before me, stays beside me, and follows after me. I accepted the invitation.

When the day arrived, there were a lot of women at the New Hope Baptist Church where the conference was held. (I thought it rather strange to hold a Muslim conference inside a Baptist church.) When the time came for me to speak, I began my talk with the greeting, "I greet you in the name of Jehovah, Yahweh, my Creator and my God, and in the name of Jeshua, Jesus Christ, my Lord and Savior." I reasoned that if they can greet assemblies by acknowledging Allah, I could greet them in the name of the Lord. Boy, you could have heard a pin drop. But I had set the stage for who I am in Christ.

I proceeded to talk about my marriage of thirty-six years and how God had brought us out of some of the pitfalls of marriage; how I had to call on Jesus all the time to help me; how the Holy Spirit had guided me with the kind of wisdom I could not possibly have gotten from within myself; how they too could have the blessing of this kind of wisdom; how biblical wisdom yields peace and joy; how the joy of the Lord destroys hostility and bitterness between spouses and spills over into the community. Frequently while I was speaking, many of the women shouted out in agreement with what I was saying. There were spurts of applause, and by the end of my speech, women were standing up all over the sanctuary happily nodding their heads, waving their handkerchiefs, clapping their hands, saying, "Yes! Speak on, Sister. Tell the truth!" I cannot tell you if they fully accepted the truth that Jesus Christ is the Messiah and Savior of all humankind. I can tell you that they did not reject outright what I was saying. Many of them thanked me for such a powerful message.

Before I went to the conference I'd spent a lot of time in prayer. I asked the Lord to help me speak and act in love and peace. I didn't want to do anything that would negatively affect my Christian witness to those Muslim women. I prayed that God's ministering angels would be there to help me do my Master's will. God heard my prayers and granted abundant grace. My friend tells me that her daughter and other members of Mohammad's Mosque are still talking about how encouraging and enlightening my words were to them. Glory to God!

Now I have a pending invitation to speak for a Jewish conference. I don't know what I'm going to talk about or how I will approach it, but I do know this: Wherever God leads me, he will give me the wisdom to represent him rightly. I also have come to realize that all people are born with an innate desire to be in fellowship with the Creator. The world is looking for God in so many different places. Christians have been given a mandate to go into all the world and preach the gospel to every creature, and I accept that mandate as my own. God gives me opportunities to represent him, not because I'm so wonderful and know so much, but because I'm willing and available for him to use me.

Sometimes it feels scary to address people with beliefs so different from my own, but I count it a blessing and privilege to be entrusted with such strategic assignments. I delight in the words of the prophet Isaiah:

> How beautiful on the mountains
> are the feet of those who bring good news,
> who proclaim peace,
> who bring good tidings,
> who proclaim salvation,
> who say to Zion, "Your God reigns!"
>
> ISAIAH 52:7

*Father, the whole world is looking for a relationship with you, whether the people know it or not. Some look to various religions, cults, customs, traditions, works; but, praise God, you have provided the way through your Son, Jesus Christ. Even when your Son's name is used in places where it's not popular, people have to take notice that his presence is there. You do reign over every place, person, principality, purpose, and possibility, and you provide a forum for the truth to be revealed. Thank you that your children can say with confidence, "Our God reigns!" Amen.*

## All Messed Up

It is only God that may be had for the asking.
LOWELL

Once upon a time, almighty God looked upon an unformed mass and said, "I'm going to make a world."

So he made the birds and the bees, the flowers and the trees, the stars up above . . . and a thing called LOVE! And that was good!

Then, when he wanted someone who could speak the language of his heart and have sweet fellowship with him, he made a man and a woman. But they became arrogant and wanted to be as smart as God, so they disobeyed his simple instructions for how to live happily ever after. They messed up. So God threw them out of their magnificent Garden home.

God's first people bore a lot of children, but they were all disobedient just like their parents. They messed up. So God did away with them all, except his servant Noah, Noah's family, and a menagerie of birds and beasts.

At first Noah was very grateful for God's favor. Noah followed God's instructions to the letter and built an ark. Noah was doubly grateful when his ark sailed through the deadly flood God sent to destroy everything on the earth. But when the rains stopped, Noah got drunk and messed up with God.

God then thought, "I know someone I can trust to be the father of many nations. Maybe he'll understand how much I love him, and perhaps he'll do the right thing."

So God chose Abraham as his own. But Abe got impatient, had a baby by a woman other than his wife, and messed up with God. God still loved him though, and in his grace he finally gave Abraham the son he'd promised.

Abraham's son Isaac wasn't perfect either. Neither was Isaac's son Jacob. One by one they kept messing up with God.

So God anointed priests. They messed up. He gave authority to judges. They messed up. He sent the prophets. They all messed up.

I can just hear God saying, "If you want something done right, you've got to do it yourself." So God put on the skin of a man and came to earth to live, love, and die so that every messy person could have perfect fellowship with him.

That's called grace incarnate. When God sent his Son, Jesus, to live among us and die for our sins, he knew we did not and never would deserve this kind of sacrificial love. But he also knew we would continue to mess up until the end of time. We could never save ourselves, so he poured out his life for us and brought us back into the Garden of his love.

What a gift! Knowing that God's Son died a cruel death on an old rugged cross so that I can have an intimate relationship with the Almighty makes me want to reach out my short, chubby arms, grab Jesus around his neck, and hug him the way my grandchildren hug me tight and say, "Grammy, I love you!" Even when they've misbehaved, they can come to me and steal my heart with their sweet embrace.

When we embrace the grace of God, we can come to him with the spirit of a little child and say, "Father, I've messed up. Please forgive me. I love you!" Instantly, faster than a grandmother's pardon, God grants us his unmerited favor through Christ Jesus and loves us freely once more.

What a gift! When you mess up, God's there to clean you up. Just run to him with your arms open wide. He'll return your embrace every time.

*The LORD, the LORD, the compassionate and gracious God, slow to anger, abounding in love and faithfulness, maintaining love to thousands, and forgiving wickedness, rebellion and sin.*

EXODUS 34:6–7

## Grace Period

> Our failure is frightful, our falling inglorious, our dying
> wretched. Yet never does love's compassionate eye turn
> from us, nor the operation of mercy cease.
>
> JULIAN OF NORWICH

My husband, George, and I were blessed with financial comfort from the day we married, April Fools' Day 1961, until the year 1986. During that time, we never had a bill collector call us or have threats flood our mailbox. We were always able to buy much of what we wanted. When our children were small, I was a stay-at-home mom. When they started kindergarten, I went back to work, not because I had to but because I wanted to. I was a bank officer at the largest independent bank in Texas, where I had clout, prestige, authority, insurance, and a paycheck. Thangs were purty.

In 1980, I decided to go into the speaking business for myself. Teaching for the American Institute of Banking had opened the door for me to be a frequent speaker for financial institutions across the country. My business was firmly established by 1984 when I resigned from the bank to be a full-time entrepreneur. My calendar was full with speaking engagements and long-term training contracts. Money was no object because I was making plenty of it—until 1986!

You know what happened. Banks started failing and falling like flies. Within six weeks after the worm turned, I lost all my speaking contracts as Texas banks tumbled.

Outside banking I had no credibility, but not being one of faint heart, I thought I was good enough to market myself fast enough to be on my feet in short order. Not! For one year, I cold-called, beat the pavement, mailed brochures, joined networking organizations, wrote a column for a neighborhood newspaper, socialized, fraternized, and did everything in my power to get work. Nothing worked!

By now, money was running out. I had overextended myself during the good times and run up the balances on my credit cards. I now was on a first-name basis with several bill collectors.

Even though I had written to all my creditors and explained our situation, it didn't help when I had to take their calls. So I took advantage of my situation and their time to present Jesus in some way. When a collector called, I would ask if he or she had ever been in my situation. Sometimes my question would spark conversation. Other times the collector would become hostile and rude. In either case, I'd listen, then give what I thought would be a friendly and appropriate response. I actually started to count it a blessing from God that my unpleasant financial situation gave me the opportunity to talk to these people. I had a working telephone that could be used to help bring people into the kingdom!

During that period of financial drought, God led three of those creditors to extend grace to me. Two allowed my good credit rating to stand while I continued to make small monthly payments. One creditor just stopped sending bills. Thirteen years ago, they just stopped coming!

I've heard of a grace period for paying bills, but I'd never heard of a grace decade for a debt owed. That creditor exonerated me. All my creditors were lenient. Oh, what grace!

I did not deserve the goodness I received. It was granted, though, in spite of me. Good times returned. There were new contracts. Cash flowed again. I paid my bills and began to get on my feet again. Everything I thought I had lost during that down time has been regained, and more.

My creditors gave me favor, mercy, forgiveness, compassion, tolerance, and pardon. My debts were finally paid. In full.

And my creditors' grace is only a flicker of the splendor of God's grace toward each of us. When you and I overextended ourselves in sin and owed a debt we could not pay, Jesus paid it in full on the cross of Calvary by shedding his blood, dying, and rising again. Through his blood, we are granted complete pardon and total salvation. We did nothing to deserve it. Because he wanted an intimate relationship with us that could not exist until our debt was paid, our Father sent his only Son to pay off our account. In full.

Marvelous, infinite, matchless grace! It's yours, my friend. Receive it.

*For Christ died for sins once for all, the righteous for the unrighteous, to bring you to God.*

1 PETER 3:18

*Lost and Found*

> We have to realize that we cannot earn
> or win anything from God; we must either receive it
> as a gift or do without it.
> OSWALD CHAMBERS

I've always been fascinated with one of the most colorful women in the Bible—Rahab, the heroine of Jericho. Jericho was the key to the Israelites' conquest of the Promised Land. If Joshua was going to defeat the enemies of God's children in Canaan, he had to get Jericho first. The people of Jericho were keenly aware of this and had fortified themselves with weapons and soldiers to protect their city. Joshua had to send in spies to scope out what the Israelite army would be up against if they tried to take the city.

When Joshua sent two men from Acacia to spy on Jericho, they went to Rahab's home. She was a woman of ill repute, a prostitute. It was not unusual to see men going in or out of her house. Little did anyone suspect that Rahab the harlot had been tagged by God to play a special role in the unfolding of his plan.

Rahab welcomed the spies and hid them from the king of Jericho and his men. When the soldiers came to Rahab's house to ask about the men who had been there, Rahab said, "Yes, the men came to me, but I did not know where they had come from. At dusk, when it was time to close the city gate, the men left. I don't know which way they went. Go after them quickly. You may catch up with them" (Josh. 2:4–5).

Actually, the Jewish spies were hiding on the roof of Rahab's house at that very moment. But when Rahab sent the king's men in the wrong direction, they believed her story and hurriedly left to look for their enemies outside the city. In exchange for her courageous protection of them and her faith in their God, the spies struck a deal with Rahab, promising to spare her and her family when Joshua's army came back to destroy Jericho.

The thing that most fascinates me about this story is that God used this Canaanite woman, this black woman from the ancestry of Ham, this woman with a bad reputation and immoral profession, to prove that his grace is sufficient for anyone and everyone. His mercy is bestowed on all who repent. His salvation is freely given to all who confess him as Lord and receive him as Master of their lives. For her whole life, Rahab had been lost in the wilderness of sin. But now she was found by a loving heavenly Father who honored her heart and not only saved her life but named her proudly in the genealogy of Jesus Christ (Matt. 1:5; Heb. 11:31).

You see, sweetie, God makes no distinction on account of nationality, race, caste, or gender. He made us all and loves us equally. Christ came to remove every last wall of partition between us and his Father so that everybody who wants to can become part of his family. God's plan is for all of us to turn from our wicked ways and worship him like his daughter Rahab did. Even though we disobey his law, he has chosen to redeem us under the new covenant of Jesus Christ. As he rescued Rahab, not only from death but also from the clutches of her own sin, so he plans to rescue each one of us from our fate apart from him. "The Lord is not slow in keeping his promise, as some understand slowness. He is patient with you, not wanting anyone to perish, but everyone to come to repentance" (2 Peter 3:9).

Dear friend, if you are lost, you can be found. No one is destined for the "unclaimed" bin at life's Lost and Found. Simply acknowledge your need for the Savior and honor God as Rahab did. It doesn't matter who you are or where you've been. That's why grace is so amazing. It saves wretches like Rahab, like me, like you. Receive the gift, dear one. You are welcome in the family.

*There is neither Jew nor Greek, slave nor free, male nor female, for you are all one in Christ Jesus.*

GALATIANS 3:28

## Stormy Weather

Faith is a living, daring confidence in God's grace,
so sure and certain that a man would stake
his life on it a thousand times.

MARTIN LUTHER

It was a beautiful, cloudless, calm afternoon on the beach at the Radisson Normandy Hotel in San Juan, Puerto Rico. It was the kind of day that makes you want to relax, read a good book, and soak in the sun. All conditions were right for a perfectly peaceful afternoon.

I settled into my beach chair with a good book, occasionally sipping tea through a red straw from a tall glass filled with ice chips, an orange wedge, a cherry, and a sprig of mint. Life was ever so sweet . . . for about an hour.

Suddenly the wind began to blow. The sky quickly changed from blue to gray to black. The storm was coming in so fast that I grabbed my book and my tea and hurried toward the verandah. I didn't make it. The rain started falling in sheets.

My greatest concern was my hair. See, I can't get my hair wet and shake it back to life like half the people in the world can. Black hair don't shake back, baby. You gotta go through a complex process to make it presentable.

Once I reached the verandah, I felt safer. I was a little disappointed, but I reasoned that I could still relax in a lawn chair on the verandah.

Just as I settled in and began reading, however, the wind changed direction. The rain started spraying in my face like water spewing out of a showerhead.

Man! Dragging my drenched tail into my small, but elegant, hotel room, I flounced grumpily on the bed and demanded, "What's going on, Lord?" All I wanted was peace and quiet with birds chirping in the nearby trees and the sound of gentle waves rolling on the shore. Was that really too much to ask?

*So now what should I do?* I could go downstairs to the bar. But someone might think I was there to be picked up. I could go to the Plaza of the Americas and shop, but I had asked God to help get me out of credit card debt. Besides, I didn't really *need* anything. I could go to the restaurant again—the one I had just left. But they might think I had an eating (or drinking) disorder. Maybe I should just stay in my room and take a nap.

As I finished weighing my options, I looked out of the window and saw that as suddenly as the rains had come, the wind had ceased, the sun had returned, and all was calm again. And in the distant sky was a faint rainbow. Man!

That's the way it is with life. Things may be going well. You may be enjoying luxuries and success, prestige and power, good health and prosperity. Then storms roll in with sudden vengeance, and your ship begins to sink.

Jesus' disciples knew all about scary storms. One day Jesus and his friends set sail across the Sea of Galilee to relax. Suddenly, without warning, the winds changed and big waves began breaking over the boat, filling it with water. Frightened, the disciples went to Jesus, who was asleep in the back of the boat.

What! Asleep? They were indignant! Terrified! They woke him up and demanded to know, "Teacher, don't you care if we drown?"

Jesus was cool. He turned to the elements and said, "Quiet! Be still!"

Then he turned back to his disciples and asked two poignant questions: "Why are you so afraid?" And, "Do you still have no faith?" (Mark 4:37–40).

The disciples didn't get it. Even though they had been with Jesus when he had changed the water to wine, healed the sick, given sight to the blind, and opened deaf ears, here they were allowing the wind and big waves to frighten them, even though the Savior was with them.

But don't be too hard on the disciples. Every day we are blessed with opportunities to unwrap God's grace in our scary moments. Every day we witness miracles that we know no human could perform—miracles like being able to breathe, walk, talk, move, see, think, taste, and touch. Evidence of God's presence and power is all around us in the universe—the sun, the stars, the birth of each new day. And yet, like Jesus' friends of old, we continue to search for peace outside of him, even when he is with us moment by moment on our journey. We sometimes ask the same question the disciples did: "Who is this?" (Mark 4:41).

Well, let's unwrap the gift he is to us.

He's someone we can pray to.
He knows what we need before we ask.
He keeps his promises.
He's our example.
He understands our fears.
He's always near.
He's our bridge over troubled waters.
He commands, "Quiet! Be still!"

When stormy weather rolls in around you, cry out to Jesus. No climactic change in your life is distressing or surprising to him. Listen to his still small voice as he whispers to you, "Why are you so afraid? Do you still have no faith?" When the gale is raging, you can be assured that he is standing by, speaking peace to your soul. Even the wind and the waves obey his will.

*Their ships are tossed to the heavens and sink again to the depths; the sailors cringe in terror. They reel and stagger like drunkards and are at their wit's end. Then they cry to the Lord in their trouble, and he saves them. He calms the storm and stills the waves. What a blessing is that stillness, as he brings them safely into harbor!*

PSALM 107:26–30 TLB

# *Granny's Grace*

We are raised high in God's sight through his grace. . . .
For our courteous Lord does not wish his creatures
to lose hope even if they fall frequently and grievously;
for our failure does not prevent him from loving us.

JULIAN OF NORWICH

When I was a little girl, I lived in an apartment with my great-great-grandmother, Grandma Mollie; Granny, my great-grandmother who raised me; and my great-grandfather, Daddy Harrell. Across the front of the entire apartment building was a screened-in front porch, and a long flight of stairs extended from our apartment to the yard below.

One sunny, hot day, I was sitting on the porch talking to Daddy Harrell. Granny was working in her flower garden downstairs, and Grandma Mollie was enjoying her afternoon tobacco. When Grandma Mollie decided it was time to spit, she strolled to the top of the stairs, leaned over the wooden banister, and spewed a big wad of snuff.

It landed smack dab on top of my kneeling granny's head.

Granny screeched so loud, I bet everyone in the next county heard her. "Mama!" she hollered. "Can't you see I'm down here? You spit that stuff in my hair! What'cha doing spitting off the banister anyway? You got a spit can! I just washed my hair and now I've got to wash it again.

I'm so mad at you I don't know what to do. Get back in the house. I don't even want to look at you right now!"

Grandma Mollie was soooo embarrassed. She hadn't even looked down when she stepped up to the banister. All she'd been thinking about was emptying her mouth of that accumulation of snuff. Stunned and hurt by her daughter's harsh words, Grandma Mollie slowly walked back into the house with tears beginning to trickle down her beautiful, high cheekbones.

"I didn't see her," she lamented. "I never would've done that if I'd seen her. I love her! I just didn't see her."

Mad Granny swept swiftly up the stairs with garden dirt on her hands and snuff spit on her head. By the time Granny reached the front door of the apartment, Grandma Mollie was crying openly, I was crying, and Daddy Harrell was pleading.

"Sweetie," he said, "don't be mad at Mollie. Don't be hard on her. She didn't see you. She didn't mean it. Can't you see she's as hurt as you are? Come on now, wash your hair and get over it. Sweetie, look at your mama. She's hurting because of this."

Granny looked at her mother's hurt, distraught, apologetic face, and tears of compassion began to flow down her brown, round cheeks, lapping under her double chin. In that moment I saw in my granny's eyes a love for her mother that words cannot express.

With the snuff still in her hair and dirt underneath her fingernails, Granny knelt at her mother's feet as Grandma Mollie sat in the old dark brown velveteen rocker. Granny laid her head in Grandma's lap and said, "Mama, I know you didn't mean it. I forgive you!"

What a gift! Pardon and reconciliation. Grandma Mollie unwrapped it with relief and joy.

I learned something that day about the way our Father God deals with us. Daddy Harrell showed me how Jesus, who is sitting at the right hand of his Father making intercession for us, pleads for sinners: "They're sorry, Father. Have mercy on them." My granny, willing to hear the plea of "guilty" and respond with such tenderness and pardon, was a picture of what a gracious God offers us all. We step to the banister of our lives, fail to consider the consequences of what we're about to do, and spit our selfish desires in the face of Jesus. Once we realize what we've done, we begin to plead for mercy and forgiveness. Even though he's hurt and grieved about what we've done, he listens to our plea, wraps us in his loving embrace, and grants us unmerited favor—grace that is greater than all our sin. That day on the porch I saw myself in Grandma Mollie—a recipient of the gift of grace.

Do you need grace today, my friend? Pardon and reconciliation? Amazing grace is the kind of grace we sing about. It is yours for the unwrapping. Accept the gift. Open it with joy!

*Yet he, being compassionate, forgave their iniquity, and did not destroy them; he restrained his anger often, and did not stir up all his wrath.*

PSALM 78:38 RSV

## *I Blew It*

He will continually follow you with his favours,
and not let slip any opportunity to be gracious to you.
MATTHEW HENRY

My friend in Arizona sent me an "IMPORTANT" e-mail that needed immediate action. The message said that Christians had allowed the famous atheist Madalyn Murray O'Hare to remove prayer from school and that now she was working to get Christian radio and television off the airwaves. The Federal Communications Commission had scheduled a hearing in Washington, and more than 287,000 names had already been registered approving the elimination of Christian programming. One million signatures were needed to stop this proceeding! A form letter was attached to the e-mail asking that every adult in the family sign the letter individually and that we also get our churches, neighbors, and friends to sign and send copies of the letter in protest.

Being the advocate for Christian programming on radio and television that I am, I was not about to stand back and watch this kind of thing happen again! I organized my staff to prepare 2,000 of these letters and get them in the mail that very day.

Late Friday evening, after the big push to get this information into the hands of thousands before Sunday morning so they could present this information to their churches, I received a phone call from a friend asking three simple questions:

1. Has Madalyn Murray O'Hare been found? (She had been missing for more than three years.)
2. When is the hearing scheduled?
3. Is there a specific person to send the letter to?

I promptly got back on e-mail and queried my friend in Arizona. This was her reply:

Dear Thelma,

I am soooo sorry! I recently found out the Madalyn Murray O'Hare information is a hoax! I received the e-mail from a credible source and just assumed they had checked into it. I tried to remember who all I had forwarded that e-mail to so I could let everyone know that this information is not true, but obviously I forgot that I'd sent it to you. I've learned my lesson, and am going to research more thoroughly before forwarding any more e-mails similar to this!

My stomach dropped to my feet. My head started pounding. No! No! How could I have been so gullible? Why didn't I check out the story for myself? What have I done? What will people think when they discover I sent them down the wrong path?

I prayed, "Lord, show me how to handle this because you know the damage I've done. At least two thousand people have been sent erroneous information. Just think how far it can spread!"

Karole, my administrative assistant, had worked like mad to get the letters out. I just knew she was going to be upset because I had taken her off another important project to complete this one. But when I broke the news to her, she just said, "Oh, that's all right. I only got six hundred letters sent out on Friday. The other fourteen hundred letters are still in my office. I know who the six hundred are . . . all I have to do is send them an apology."

Whew! God, in his infinite wisdom and mercy, saved us from the overwhelming embarrassment and expense of my misguided zealousness.

As Christians, we have responsibility to seek out the truth and know it for ourselves. How often do we misinterpret and misquote Scripture because we fail to go to the Bible and understand its message? How often have we led people down the wrong path because of our actions and words? It is by the grace of God that we are able to work through these situations without doing irreparable damage.

God knew the potential results of my actions before I did and graciously conceived a time delay in disseminating my "urgent" message. That's grace! My goal was to STOP THIS RIGHT NOW—by my own efforts. But who am I, without God's clear direction, to try to stop anything? I blew it. God hindered it. Grace covered it. What a gift!

When we open our eyes to the gift of grace each day, we discover that God is always working behind the scenes of our lives, covering our tracks when we hook up the cart before the horse . . . when we are so determined to do right that we fail to be reasonable.

*Great are the works of the LORD; they are pondered by all who delight in them. Glorious and majestic are his deeds, and his righteousness endures forever. He has caused his wonders to be remembered; the LORD is gracious and compassionate.*

PSALM 111:2–4

# Who's in Charge?

> God is gracious to whom he will be gracious. He is not limited by anyone's wickedness. He is never trapped by his own wrath. His grace may break out anywhere he pleases.
>
> JOHN PIPER

What an honor! Karen had asked me to speak at her church women's conference for the second consecutive year. The conference the year before had been such a special time for the women and for me, a high holy worship day in which the Lord healed and delivered.

As I prepared for the upcoming conference, I studied my Bible, took copious notes, and organized in my mind what I wanted to say and how I wanted to express it. I completed all my research and studied and defined every word I had questions about. I did everything I could think of to make this message even better than last year's. But something was missing.

The day came; the hour for speaking was nearly upon me. Even though I had studied, prepared, and rehearsed in my mind, something was still missing. Before I spoke, I asked my assistant, Pat, to pray for me because I was so unsettled. She, too, sensed that something was not right. But even her righteous prayers did not settle my spirit.

I went ahead and spoke, God moved, and people were helped. In the middle of my speech, the Holy Spirit turned the course of what I was saying into a personal testimony about my marriage. Women throughout the sanctuary were moved to tears. God clearly was in control. But something was still missing.

All the compliments and accolades I received after the message did not assuage my discomfort. The women who shared lunch with me after I spoke told me how powerful my message had been. But my spirit remained troubled.

Later that evening, I got on my knees at home and said, "Okay, God. You moved today in spite of me. But what was missing? Did I do what you wanted me to? People were helped. Marriages were saved. But I feel so very far from you. What's wrong?"

I waited on his answer, and it came to me as clear as day: "You never asked me what *I* wanted you to say. You just went out on your own without consulting me!"

The truth hit me like the proverbial ton of bricks. He was right! Not once in the course of preparing for the message did I ask God for his guidance. I simply considered the theme requested by Karen and based what I was going to say on what she said she wanted, not on what God wanted. Only after I asked for wisdom from God and took time to listen did he reveal to me what had been missing all along. After I repented, he sent a portion of peace my way.

I've always made a habit of asking for God's guidance. So what happened this time? For that, I don't have a good answer. Perhaps I got so caught up in the events of the week and the deadlines that I simply forgot who's in charge. I'm not — that's for sure! It could be that my ego was on the front burner because I wanted to surpass last year's "performance." I honestly don't know what I was thinking about instead of my Master.

God could have gotten very angry with me and decided to show me up in front of all those people by allowing me to fall flat on my face. But he didn't. My neglecting him did not deter him from doing what he wanted to do for the women at that conference. He completely revised my speech and caused words to flow from my mouth that I had never even considered saying to that crowd. Even though I had not asked for his advice, God did take control. He made good what could have ended badly.

It's amazing to me how, in spite of our natural neglect of God, he uses us for his glory. He shows up with his extravagant grace, grants us undeserved favor, and allows us to carry out what he has started.

Have you ever known in your "knower" that something was wrong, but you could not put your finger on the problem? Learn from my mistake. Ask for wisdom. If you don't hear from God immediately, pray for seven days that he will speak to you. Seven is said to be the number of completion. If you ask God sincerely in faith, believing he will answer you, he will not disappoint you.

I had to learn the hard way: "When you ask, you do not receive, because you ask with wrong motives, that you may spend what you get on your pleasures" (James 4:3). Now I make it a practice to remind myself of the liberating truth: "Thelma, trust in the LORD with all your heart and lean not on your own understanding; in all your ways acknowledge him, and he will make your paths straight" (Prov. 3:5–6). Now that's grace!

*If any of you lacks wisdom, he should ask God, who gives generously to all without finding fault, and it will be given to him.*

JAMES 1:5

# *Be Yourself*

> God has a purpose for each one of us, a work
> for each one to do, an influence for each one to exert,
> a likeness to His dear Son for each one to manifest,
> and then a place for each one to fill in His holy temple.
>
> ARTHUR C. A. HALL

What comes to mind when you think of the word *authority?* Webster's defines authority as a noun: "The power or right to command, act . . ."

But what does authority mean to a child of God?

The word *authority* has a word in it that tells the whole story: "author." Author means creator, organizer, cause, source of things. Authority is what you are authorized to do. It is the work to which you are called by God, who is the author and finisher of your faith. As a child of God, your authority is determined by God, and your authenticity is determined by how you fulfill what God has entrusted to you. Your authority is your calling, appointment, ordination, assignment, gifts, talents, and personal passion given to you by God to be carried out for his purposes. Wow!

In light of the spiritual meaning of authority, consider this: When we try to do and act like other people, we are acting in an unauthorized capacity. When we try to be someone we're not, when we try to emulate gifts, skills, and characteristics that are not ours, we abuse the authority we have been given as individuals whom God has blessed with a unique purpose.

I have the God-given authority to speak convincingly, powerfully, and boldly for the Lord. If I had the opportunity, I would get up every morning and speak somewhere. That's my passion in life. God called me to do that and continually gives me everything it takes to speak — the knowledge, the engagements, and the words to say. I love it so much that I give away a lot of time, effort, energy, and experience doing what I'm called to do without getting overly tired.

There are some things, however, that I cannot do well. I've tried, but it just doesn't work. For example, I took piano lessons for four years, trying to learn to play like one of my best friends. During that period of time, I told her how angry and frustrated I was because I was not able to play the piano like she could. In fact, I could not play the piano like *anyone* who can play. For three years I agonized over my inability to get out of Thompson's Book One. You know, the red book. For hours I would sit at my piano and attempt to make music. Instead, noise came out of it. I rationalized that it was the piano that sounded so bad, so I sold that old piano and bought a new name-brand job. Believe me, it was not the piano.

Sometimes I became so frustrated that I would literally sit at the piano and cry. One day, in the midst of my pity party, the light came on: "Thelma, why don't you ask your friend to play for you while you sing. She can play, you can't. You can sing, she can't."

What a brilliant idea! Sometimes I'm slow. It took me four years to figure out that I'd been agonizing and fretting over something that I had absolutely no "authority" over or in! God did not call me to play the piano, he called me to sing and to speak and to bear witness to his grace. I started realizing that when I'd sung at church throughout my life, entered oratorical contests all through school, and always jumped at the chance to be in front of an audience even as a little girl, God was preparing me to fulfill my "authority." My college preparation to be a teacher and my years teaching children and adults honed my God-given skills for the day when I would start my own speaking business and later speak before thousands of people in conferences all over the world.

Honey, if you are trying to be something you know you aren't, if you are trying to do things you know you have little ability, patience, passion, commitment, and tolerance for, cut it out! Be yourself! The great thing about real authority is that God gives me one thing to do, somebody else another, somebody else something else; or he may give us the same talent but have us exhibit it in different ways. Blending our authority with other people's authority creates the kind of kingdom on earth that personifies God's kingdom in heaven. The reason Lucifer was kicked out of heaven was that he tried to usurp God's authority and be something he wasn't. How very stupid when he had the fourth best position in heaven! His jealousy and rebellion cost him his position, his beauty, his ability to make angelic music, and his intimacy with God. When we operate outside of our authority, we experience similar breakdowns.

But that doesn't have to happen to you. Just be who you are, what you are, how you are, the way God made you. It is his grace that creates in you the talents, inclinations, knowledge, and *pleasure* to be yourself. Grace empowers you to perform the tasks God has given you on earth, and to enjoy what he has called you to do. And, baby, it's all just a rehearsal for when we will rule and reign with him on high!

*Now the body is not made up of one part but of many. . . . If the whole body were an eye, where would the sense of hearing be? If the whole body were an ear, where would the sense of smell be? But in fact God has arranged the parts in the body, every one of them, just as he wanted them to be.*

1 CORINTHIANS 12:14, 17–18

## Grace at Home

Learn to lavish the grace of God on others.
Be stamped with God's nature, and His blessing
will come through you all the time.

OSWALD CHAMBERS

I had been taught from kindergarten on that you should pray for what you want, and God will give it to you. Well, at the time, I didn't know that wasn't the entire picture, but I did believe that God would listen to my heart's every wish. So in my early teens I started praying for God to send me a good husband.

When George Wells walked into my Sunday school class in January of 1956, I knew before I even met him that he was the one. I waited every Sunday to see this special young man. When I turned fifteen, my granny let George come over to visit, but she sat in the living room with us while we played Chinese checkers over and over again. No hanky-panky for Thelma!

Finally, six years later, George and I were married. We've been married for nearly forty years now, and life gets sweeter every year. My husband is a man among men. My relationship with him is one where love, understanding, happiness, peace, comfort, pleasure, and intimacy are lavished upon me—no strings attached.

But George is not a saint—and neither am I. Like every other couple, we've had some rough times and we've walked on some shaky ground. People sometimes ask me what our "secret" is to staying happily married for so long. Well, there is no question in my mind that the most crucial ingredient to a successful relationship is God's grace. Grace is the glue that keeps George and me together, and it is pure gift. But God also taught us long ago to be gracious to one another. By practicing the art of extending grace at home, we have avoided many of the heartaches we've watched other couples suffer.

It wasn't always like that. In the early years of our marriage, we argued a lot. (That's a nice way of saying we were at each other's throats on too many occasions to count!) Thangs weren't purty. After one particularly vicious fight, George approached me and asked me to promise him that we would not argue again. If either of us found ourselves getting "hot under the collar," we would agree to call a "time-out" and separate until we cooled down.

With an "attitude," I agreed, thinking George would never follow through. But much to my surprise, he did just what he had suggested. The next time things started to get heated, he went out to his car and drove off until he thought I'd cooled off. I fumed up a storm while he was gone, but by the time he got back I was ready to act like an adult and talk things out rationally. Instead of continuing to inflict wound upon wound, as we'd always done, we began to respond rather than to react. Grace and peace began to reign in our home.

It's been over twenty years since George and I have had a fight. Now, I didn't say we've never been angry with each other in those twenty years; I said we haven't fought. You see, you can disagree but remain agreeable. Ruth Bell Graham's wise words apply in every marriage: "It's my job to love Billy. It's God's job to make him good."

One of my earliest "practice sessions" around this concept occurred when one of our daughters asked George if she could attend a slumber party. I'd already given her permission, never dreaming that George would say no. So we were both stunned when he said, "Absolutely not! I will not have a daughter of mine spending the night in somebody else's house. You don't know what's going on in somebody else's house."

Practicing being "agreeable" was not easy in that moment! Especially while I watched my baby cry, "Why, Daddy? Why? Why are you so mean, Daddy?" My heart was breaking for her, and I was mad enough to hit him. I could not understand his reasoning. But I read a bumper sticker once that said, "If my husband and I agreed on everything, one of us would not be necessary." I could have simply defied George's decision and let our daughter go to the slumber party or, probably even worse, scolded him in front of her. But this would hardly have created a gracious atmosphere in our home. I chose not to say anything to George until I'd cooled off a bit, comforted our daughter, and gotten my husband to myself.

As part of our pact never to have another destructive argument, George and I had agreed never to go to sleep angry with each other. As the evening wore on, I knew that pledge was about to be tested. So I prayed. As hacked off as I was, I tried to consider how I would want to be approached if I were in my husband's shoes.

Finally, right before bedtime, I sat down next to George and said, "Honey, you are a good father, and I know you would never hurt our children deliberately." Rather than telling him off, I asked him, "Tell me again why you made that decision about the slumber party. I'm just having a problem understanding it because I don't see anything wrong with it."

George vented. He laid out all his reasoning to me in detail, and by the grace of God I didn't interrupt once. But I kept praying for strength to keep still while George expressed various opinions I disagreed with at the time. Finally, I told him how much I appreciated his concern for our daughter. I also asked him to make another agreement with me for the future: when one of our children had a request, both Mom and Dad would discuss it first before making any hard-and-fast decision. George agreed.

When we got into bed that night, we weren't all lovey-dovey, but at least we had successfully broken the habit of inflicting more damage on one another whenever we disagreed. As upset as I was with George at the time, I chose to extend grace to him the way I would have wanted him to extend it to me.

Since then, my husband and I have spent decades developing a new habit: treating each other the way God treats us. And you know what? It's really not as hard as we thought it would be!

*Get rid of all bitterness, rage and anger, brawling and slander, along with every form of malice. Be kind and compassionate to one another, forgiving each other, just as in Christ God forgave you.*

EPHESIANS 4:31–32

*Flowers for Erin*

Grace is glory begun, and glory is but grace perfected.
JONATHAN EDWARDS

When I first met Sandy fifteen years ago, she was a good woman, but not a Christian. When she did receive Christ as her personal Savior, she had no idea that on January 23, 1999, she would experience the kindness of her loving heavenly Father the way she did. In fact, she told me, had he not shown her his grace in a tangible way, she didn't think she would have made it.

Early on the morning of January 20, Sandy received a call from her son, Tom, asking her to pray for his baby girl who had just been born a few minutes after midnight. Though she was four weeks early, Erin was a big baby, but she had severe internal problems.

Sandy prayed steadily. Less than twenty-four hours later, she received another call from Tom telling her, through sobs, that Erin was not doing well, and if Sandy and her husband wanted to see her before she died, they needed to leave *now*. Sandy prayed and cried for most of the five-hour trip to Detroit.

When they arrived at the hospital, Sandy saw her precious little Erin hooked up to a maze of machines and tubes. The baby looked so helpless and vulnerable. Between visits, Sandy retreated to her Bible to search for words of comfort and some clue as to why all this was happening. She came upon Jeremiah 29:11–14:

> "For I know the plans I have for you," declares the LORD, "plans to prosper you and not to harm you, plans to give you hope and a future. Then you will call upon me and come and pray to me, and I will listen to you. You will seek me and find me when you seek me with all your heart. I will be found by you," declares the LORD, "and will bring you back from captivity. I will gather you from all the nations and places where I have banished you," declares the LORD, "and will bring you back to the place from which I carried you into exile."

Sandy was sure that God had just given her a clear message: Erin would recover and be fine. But this was not to be. Little Erin was welcomed into God's loving arms later that night.

Though Sandy felt the presence of the Lord in a very constant and comforting way, she shed many tears for *her* loss that night. While she knew she hadn't really "lost" Erin (for she truly knew where the baby was), she experienced nearly overwhelming grief.

The following day was a busy one, making funeral arrangements and buying flowers. Flowers are a very important part of Sandy's life; she loves to tend her flower beds with loving care. But when she went to the florist, Sandy could only mourn the many types of flowers that she would never get to plant with Erin. She could think only of all the things she would never get to do with her granddaughter.

She asked the florist to put together an arrangement of flowers that she had in her yard at home: lilies, agapanthus, daisies, delphiniums, coneflowers, Gerber daisies, and many more. She knew there was no way any florist in Detroit could find most of those flowers. After all, it was January!

On the day of the funeral, Sandy found herself in the church alone with Erin for a few minutes. As the funeral director carried in arrangement after arrangement of flowers, Sandy saw the one she had ordered. Every flower in her yard was in that basket! "What a powerful reminder of my Father's love for me," Sandy told me, "that he would provide the most perfect flowers for my baby granddaughter the only time I would be able to give them to her."

As Sandy continued to watch the parade of flowers, she began to mourn that Erin would never have a wedding; would never be a bride. At that very moment, the funeral director carried in a vase brimming with tall white flowers. Sandy walked over to those flowers and received a most powerful message that this was indeed Erin's bridal bouquet. Erin was now the bride of Christ!

As Sandy continued to feel great sorrow for her loss, she cried to God that her grandbaby would never go on dates or to dances; she would never get an orchid corsage from a boy. Through her tears Sandy looked at the flower arrangement again, and there, right in the center of the vase, was a stem of baby orchids. "I looked at the card on the arrangement," Sandy said, "only to find yet another hug from God. The flowers were from my two most special friends from my Bible study back home. No matter where I turned, no matter what direction my grief was taking, God was there so personally to prove to me that he knew what and how I was feeling, and *all* of the comfort he had to give was available for me in that moment. All I had to do was stop and listen."

On January 23, 1999, Sandy understood Jeremiah 29:11–14 in a new light. She saw the plans God had for her Erin. They were plans to give her a future, a future filled with beauty and happiness as his bride. "And the plans he has for me?" Sandy said. "I find bits and pieces of them daily, and I am constantly amazed at his originality in presenting them to me. When I have eyes to see, I receive endless gifts of grace to cherish and celebrate."

My friend, God's grace shows up in *all* our circumstances if we would but recognize it. When we experience grief and sorrow and things don't turn out the way we want them to, God has not left us. He gives us more and more grace when the burdens are greater and greater.

There are times in all of our lives when grief of some kind sweeps over our soul, and we find ourselves looking for answers and comfort. Isn't it wonderful to know that a loving God cares enough about what we're going through to reach down and stroke our brow, or hug us through the arms of other people, or kiss us with the sweetness of kind words. Or send us flowers. As my friend Barbara Johnson says, "God will wrap you in his comfort blanket." Let him hold you now.

*Grace and peace be yours in abundance. Praise be to the God . . . [who] has given us new birth into a living hope . . . and into an inheritance that can never perish, spoil or fade. . . . In this you greatly rejoice, though now for a little while you may have had to suffer grief in all kinds of trials. These have come so that your faith . . . may be proved genuine and may result in praise, glory and honor when Jesus Christ is revealed.*

1 PETER 1:2–7

## For the Sake of Love

Your mother didn't give you away, she just let me keep you for a while."

After a half century, those words still ring in my mind. What a wise woman my great-grandmother (Granny) was to tell me that over and over until I knew, without a doubt, that my mother had not "given me away" because she didn't love me. She only wanted to make life easier for me than it was for her.

Granny took me in when I was two years old because both my mother and I were ill. Someone needed to nurse me back to health. So Granny did, and my mother was happy and relieved.

One day when I was in elementary school, I remember going to spend the night with my mom. In fact, it is the only time I remember spending the night with her. Maybe I did other times, but if so they didn't have enough significance to remain in my memory. This time did.

My mother and baby sister lived on Starks Street in South Dallas. They lived in a tent. Yes, a camping tent. I had gone camping before during summer retreats with my church, but I had never seen anyone live in a tent day to day. What a shock!

Inside the tent were two cots. Not beds—army cots (the ugly green kind with the wooden legs that cross and fold like a big purse). Later that night I discovered that my mother slept on one cot and my sister slept on the other. *Where's the bathroom?* I thought. *No bathroom! How will I be able to use the bathroom?* This thought haunted me until the time came and neighbors were kind enough to allow me to use theirs. Inside the tent, there was no stove, just a few sticks on the ground and a big black pot over a wood fire.

My sister and I played until bedtime. *How can both of us sleep on that little cot?* I wondered. I *really* wanted to go home—home to my granny. I was getting very sad. But I didn't want my mother to feel bad, so I didn't say anything.

When we went to bed, I lay very, very still. I was afraid of falling off the cot or pushing my little sister off. The floor was dirt. No rug. No linoleum. Nothing but the hard, earthen floor.

I tried to keep my mother from hearing me cry. As quietly as I could I would sniffle and try to wipe my eyes and nose without drawing attention to myself. All I could think was, *This bed is so gritty. I want to go home where the sheets are white, clean, and pressed. I hate this place. I want to go home so I can eat some good food. I can't stand this place. I want to go home where we have rugs on the floor. I feel so dirty. I want to go home so I can bathe. Why did Granny let me come here? I want to go home!!!*

I don't think my mother slept much that night either. She was a proud lady, and I'm sure she was embarrassed and humiliated about her living conditions. Determined to never ask for a handout, she did what she could to make it in life. Hard times with no work or assistance had driven her to living the best she could, and for a very brief period, that was under the roof of this tent. Because she was crippled in her right hand and foot, my mother had difficulty convincing prospective employers to hire her. While she had more strength in her good left hand than most of us have in both of ours, many people saw only her physical deformities rather than her many abilities and skills.

When morning came, my mother spoke to me in the kindest, sweetest tone. She said, "Thelma, baby, this is no place for you. You need to go home."

That's all I needed to hear! I went to the neighbor's house and asked to use the bathroom again—and the telephone. I called Granny and told her that I needed to come home *now*. She immediately called my grandfather, Daddy Lawrence (her son and my mother's father), to come get me. He came.

Much to his surprise, he saw for the first time how his daughter and granddaughter were living. It broke his heart. He told my mother he would always be there for her. I don't know exactly how things turned around, but I do know that my mother never lived in a tent again. At first, she got a job working for a laundry and cleaning company. Then she worked for Goodwill Industries of Dallas and received awards and commendations for excellence.

As I think back on that experience, I'm reminded of two women in the Bible who were claiming to be the mother of the same boy. (You can read this amazing story in 1 Kings 3:16–28.) In order to settle the dispute, King Solomon told his servants to cut the boy in two and give each woman a half. The real mother of the boy immediately cried in horror, "Please, my lord, give her the living baby! Don't kill him!" (v. 26). Her love for her son was so strong that she would never have allowed him to be destroyed just so she could "keep" him.

I'm sure that's the way my mother felt on that desperate, demoralizing, belittling morning after hearing me quietly sob during the night. She'd rather see me clean, happy, and content with Granny than have me face the ordeals of life like she and my sister were experiencing.

Now that I'm a mother and a grandmother and reflect on that time in my family's life, I don't know if I would have been able to part with either of my children, whatever the circumstances. However, you cannot measure the length someone will go to make things right for the ones they love, including giving them up for the sake of love.

In fact, that's exactly what God did. He gave up his only Son when he sent him down to earth to experience the cruelties and difficulties of life, to literally sacrifice his body in the most humiliating death possible, to give sinners the means to come home and live with him forever. If that's not an outrageous plan to demonstrate his utterly boundless love, I don't know what is.

Few passages in Scripture sum up the glorious love of God and how far he is willing to go for us like Ephesians 3:17–19 (TLB). It is my prayer for you as you bathe in the unfathomable depths of God's love in the pages ahead.

> May your roots go down deep into the soil of God's marvelous love; and may you be able to feel and understand, as all God's children should, how long, how wide, how deep, and how high his love really is; and to experience this love for yourselves, though it is so great that you will never see the end of it or fully know or understand it. And so at last you will be filled up with God himself.

Hallelujah!

A good mother's love for her child is a classic example of Christ's love for us. You will never have a better parent than almighty God!

## No Flies in Africa

Have you ever said something that you weren't proud of and found yourself eating your words? On March 12, 2000, I had to eat my words. At least forty people in the Truth Seekers Sunday school class at St. John Missionary Baptist Church had heard me say more than once, "I just can't totally commit myself to the Lord, because he might send me to Africa, and I don't like flies!"

Can you believe that? I had been the teacher of this class for more than a decade. I studied God's Word every week and lived a Christian life, yet I was not totally committed to turning my life over to God's will. Why? Because he might send me to a mission field, and I don't like flies.

Wanna know a secret? Each time I'd make that statement, the Holy Spirit would convict me and I'd feel guilty. But I'd say it again. I said it for years. It was only after a year of struggle that I finally completely and totally gave my life over to the Lord and said, "Whatever, Lord. Send me."

And the Lord sent me to Ghana, West Africa.

What an experience! I didn't have a clue that people lived in such deplorable poverty. I've traveled to many parts of the world and have seen extreme poverty, but nothing like this. Even the largest cities are impoverished. The "haves" have a lot; the "have-nots" have little or nothing. Sanitary conditions are virtually nonexistent, and clean water is a luxury. Experiencing this has given me a greater sense of appreciation for the things most of us take for granted, such as:

hot and cold running water
flushing toilets
nutritious meals
sanitized beds and bed linens
ice
comfortable housing
radios, television, telephones, cell phones, computers
air-conditioning
washers, dryers, dry cleaning
health and medical resources
paved streets and signal lights
job and career opportunities
modern educational facilities

I could go on, but you get the picture.

I'm really glad God sent me to Africa. Not only did it open my eyes to the conditions of that land, but it also proved again God's lavish love for me. I learned that he never sends us anywhere before he has gone before and cleared the way. I went to Africa, and I don't remember being bothered once by flies. I returned home saying, "There are no flies in Africa."

Do you see why I had to eat my words? I'm certain there are flies in Africa, but they didn't bother me. When I stop to think about that, my heart leaps for joy at how God's love shows up in spite of myself. Even when I should have been committing myself to him without reservation, he put up with me and allowed me to stay healthy and strong so I could get to the place I dreaded and realize his over-the-top grace. Now I can sing this old hymn with a clean, clear, committed heart:

*All to Jesus I surrender,*
*All to him I freely give;*
*I will ever love and trust him,*
*In his presence daily live.*
*All to Jesus I surrender,*
*Make me, Savior, wholly thine;*
*May thy Holy Spirit fill me,*
*May I know thy pow'r divine.*
*All to Jesus I surrender,*
*Lord, I give myself to thee;*
*Fill me with thy love and power,*
*Let thy blessing fall on me.*
*I surrender all, I surrender all.*
*All to thee, my blessed Savior,*
*I surrender all.*

Once I surrendered all to Jesus, I found his love to be lavish. He does not stop loving us when we don't surrender to him; we just miss out on some of the blessings he longs to give us. But when we do surrender, he pours out his blessings; he helps us through tough situations; he covers our mistakes and forgives our every sin. He is patient and kind with us. Even when he disciplines us, the punishment is not what we actually deserve. His love is so lavish and free that even when we blow him off, he is steadfast. Look what he did for me! He accepted my repentance, charted my path to the place I said I didn't want to go, and kept me safe, healthy, happy, and productive while there.

Take it from me: Don't waste time holding yourself back from completely surrendering to God. God is love. He made you. He'll keep you. He won't give up on you. He has plans for you that will not harm you, but will give you a bright and glorious future.

The next time you sing, "I Surrender All," let it be the truth. He's waiting for you to surrender all to him so he can shower you with abundance!

*Our courteous Lord does not wish his creatures to lose hope even if they fall frequently and grievously; for our failure does not prevent him loving us.*

JULIAN OF NORWICH

## The Fetish Priest

Last February, when a number of us associated with Women of Faith took a trip to Ghana, our goal was to help World Vision meet the needs of the villagers. I had just finished meeting the family I had signed up to sponsor through World Vision when our language interpreter, Cecilia, asked if I wanted to visit the shrine of the fetish priest.

*Fetish priest?* I wondered with some trepidation. *What's a fetish priest? Is he a devil worshiper? Will he try to harm us?* Internally I asked myself these questions, but I simply replied, "Yes."

My new World Vision "family" — Charles and his wife and three children — are Christians. They believe in the matchless name of Jesus. But Charles's father does not. He is the chief of the village and the priest of the ancestral religion most of the residents practice. They believe that the souls of animals and other ancestral spirits can cast spells or work magic. They sacrifice animals in worship to empower the spirits to help them. In essence, they are idol worshipers.

Cecilia told me that the fetish priest was angry with his son for becoming a Christian and not following their ancestral religion. When Charles found Christ, his father despised him for it, she said. In fact, the villagers think that Charles lost his eyesight over a year ago because his father put a spell on him to make him turn back to his old religion.

As we began our short walk across the red clay dirt to the shrine, I really didn't have any fear. I just prayed in my heart that Jesus' blood would cover us and protect us. When we arrived at the shrine, there were bones, dried blood, a disturbing odor, and other evidences of animal sacrifice. Whew! Fear was all over Cecilia. She was shaking, her voice was trembling, her eyes were wide. Me, I just walked up to the shrine, greeted the priest in the name of Jehovah, our Creator, and Jesus Christ, our Savior. Because protocol is very important to the villagers, I also acknowledged the priest as chief and Charles's father.

Amazingly, I had absolutely no inhibitions as I started telling him that Jesus Christ is the Paschal Lamb who paid the price for human sin on Calvary so that we would never again have to make a blood sacrifice of an animal. I told Charles's father that the thorns that were placed on Jesus' head caused his head to bleed for *him,* the fetish priest. The blood from the nails hammered into Christ's hands was shed for him too. The blood that poured from Jesus' feet when the spikes were driven through was shed for all of us so that we would never again have to depend on the blood of an animal for help.

Cecilia was trembling so bad I wondered if she was really interpreting for him what I was saying. But the priest was definitely listening. I wondered whether he understood English. He seemed to comprehend exactly what I was saying.

I asked the priest what he wanted most in life. He replied, "I want peace. I'm worried about my son who is blind. I cannot sleep at night worrying about him."

Peace. *Isn't that what we all want?* I thought.

I replied, "Peace can be yours right this minute because we have the Peace Maker, Jesus Christ, here with us. He shed his precious blood so you could have peace. If you accept him as your Savior right now, I promise you he will place peace in your heart. You will be able to lie down without worrying about Charles, just as Charles is now able to lie down in peace. I have not seen any greater faith than that of your son and his wife. Will you accept Jesus who promises peace?"

I waited for Cecilia to finish translating what I'd said. The priest just nodded his head but did not indicate acceptance. I offered him a challenge: "If you don't accept today, will you promise me that when Charles regains his sight, this will be a sign to you that Jesus is real and you will accept him then?"

He made the sign of the cross. I interpreted that as "Yes."

I firmly believe that God is going to restore Charles's sight by either proper medical treatment or a miracle. I firmly believe that God is drawing Charles's father to himself, along with everyone in the Duabone village.

God is so organized. His timing is perfect. That very morning—Friday, February 26, 2000—I wrote this prayer in my journal:

Lord, today is the day we go into the village and visit our families who are a part of the Family Sponsorship Project. At dinner last night, I accepted the responsibility to care for a family of five with a blind father. Today, Lord, is your day to shine through me. Please, Sir, give me the words to say, the articulation to say them, and the proper interpretation of your Word. Then let your Word be welcomed by the family.

O Lord, our Lord, how excellent is your name in all the earth! I honor you with my whole heart. Thank you for this opportunity to serve you in my mother country. Lord, please help me to express how I really feel about this land, this experience, this opportunity, this hope. Let love abound in this place. Lord, please cover me with your blood. Please protect all of us from diseases, lice, bites, food poisoning, water contamination, and all other forms of sickness, hurt, harm, and danger. Father, in the name of Jesus, I denounce witchcraft, superstition, the occult, divination, libation, animism, and all other gods and demon worship in Jesus' name. I plead the blood in the Name that is above all other names. The matchless blood of Jesus is on us today. Take me out of me and replace me with you. Amen.

God did it! He replaced what could have been a spirit of fear with a heart of love.

You don't have to go to Africa and speak to a fetish priest to need fearless love. You might be going through a scary situation right now, right in your own heart. But God has not given you a spirit of fear, "but of power, and of love, and of a sound mind" (2 Tim. 1:7 KJV). So recite 1 John 4:18 over and over again: "There is no fear in love. But perfect love drives out fear." And then, my dear sisters, walk boldly forth in fearless love.

When faith is small and hope doubts, love conquers. We never have to live in fear because God's love is perfect!

# *What's in a Name?*

Have you ever been driving along and seen something that caused you to do a double take? *Whah. . . ? What was that?* That's the way it was for me when I visited Ghana.

It started when I noticed a sign on a taxi in front of us: "Jesus Cares Taxi." *Okay,* I thought. *You're right. He does care. That's nice that the cab owner recognizes that.* But as I looked out the window to my right, I saw another sign. Then I noticed other vans and vehicles passing us with all kinds of Christian wording and Scriptures written on them.

*That's odd,* I thought. *We don't do anything like this in America. Why do they do this?* I realize that our cultures are very, very different. But who ever heard of writing stuff like that all over cars and buildings? *Can't they think of something better to name their businesses?* I wondered. *Are they fanatics, or what? Has someone ordered them to do this?*

I saw so many signs that I started writing them down. My personal mission became to record as many of these signs as possible. But I saw so many words and phrases that expressed people's praise and thanksgiving to God that my hand grew tired of writing before I'd recorded a fraction of what I witnessed.

As we drove through downtown Accra, the capital of Ghana, I saw still more signs. I finally asked our World Vision host, Agnes, why the people did this.

"Christians in Ghana love the Lord and want everyone to know it," she replied. "This is our way of spreading the gospel. We want to carry the message of the saving power of Jesus Christ everywhere we go. We want to praise him in all we do, and we want people to know that we bless the Lord at all times. Some people believe that if they name their businesses after the Lord, they will be successful. Also, others display these signs as evidence that they denounce other religions, because God is greater."

The ride from Accra to Kumaski to Atebubu to Coast Cape was a challenge. Picture me riding along, bumping and bouncing up and down over the dirt roads and jungle terrain, frantically recording all the signs I saw on shacks, dumpsters, modest businesses, and cars. Would you dare name your business one of these sixty names I saw in Ghana, even though you love the Lord?

1. Nant Nante Yie (Walk Well with the Lord)
2. Nhyira Nka Boafo (Blessed Be My Helper)
3. Blessed Beauty Shop
4. Garden of Eden Sports Shop
5. Mustard Seed Prayer Center
6. Oh! Yes Jesus (bus)
7. Salon De Hope
8. Baby Jesus Nursery School
9. God Is Able Fashion Center
10. End Times Professional Studio
11. Peace Art Store
12. Nso Ya (Nothing is too difficult for God. When you get him, you are satisfied!)
13. Jesus of the Deep Forest Books
14. God's Time = Mere (The Best Time)

15. Pentecost Fire (taxi)
16. Oh Jesus! (taxi)
17. Emmanuel (a common name used on many businesses and vehicles)
18. God Is So Good (retail store)
19. Ays Fa Firi Wo (Father Forgive Them)
20. Divine Love Art Centre
21. The Merciful Lion Photographs (photos on tombstones)
22. Thank U Jesus (retail store)
23. God Is So Wonderful Fashions
24. Prince of Peace Snacks
25. The Name of the Lord Is a Strong Tower New Hope Farm
26. El Shaddai (Lord God Almighty) Center
27. Adoni (age to age you're still the same by the power of your name) Complex
28. King Jesus Cares Nursery
29. Peace and Love Shop
30. All Hail the Power of Jesus' Name (business)
31. Blessed Assurance (business)
32. All Creation Praise Jehovah (truck)
33. Jesus Saves Pharmacy
34. In God's Time Electrical Repair
35. Jesus Never Fails (truck)
36. God Is Able International
37. God's Will Coke-a-Cola
38. Nothing but the Blood Barber Shop
39. Calvary Blood Tonic
40. Zion Car Wash Shop
41. My Dawn Restaurant
42. Father Into Thy Hands I Commit My Spirit (truck)
43. Who Is Free Fashions

44. Victory Electrical Works
45. Father Abraham Construction, Ltd.
46. Heavenly Fashion and Bridal Design
47. Savior Plumbing Works
48. Dr. Jesus Bread Stand
49. Follow Me to Jesus (truck)
50. God First Beauty Shop
51. God Never Fails Building Supply
52. Peace and Love Electrical
53. New Generation Plumbing
54. Clap for Jesus Coke-a-Cola
55. Heaven's Snacks
56. Almighty Plywood and Nails
57. Christ Is My Redeemer Beauty Shop
58. Have Faith Drug Store
59. Providence (business)
60. God Is Good Hair Cuts

Ain't these names outlandish? What if this caught on in America? What if Burger King changed its name to "The Lord's Supper Burgers"? What if the Hyatt changed its name to the "Heavenly Rest with Jesus Hotel"? Imagine an automatic door or gate company called "The Pearly Gates Are Open Door Company." What if a home builder named his company "You've Got a Mansion Just Over the Hilltop"? Would we think they were a little bit nuts? Probably.

But we may need to ask ourselves, *What's in a name?* I named my company "A Woman of God Ministries." I actually felt a little embarrassed using that name. I considered how people might view me. Would they think I'm self-righteous? Think about it: What if someone handed you a business card that said, "A Woman of God." Would you question her intent?

For a time I did struggle with that name for fear of being misunderstood, but I finally accepted it as a gift. Let me explain:

In early October 1995, at the insistence of my daughter Vikki, we went to visit a local television station to investigate the possibility of producing a Christian television program. While we were there, things happened very fast and I found myself signing a year's contract to produce a program that I had no name or format for and no experience producing. The station manager's assistant, Paulette, escorted us into the studio, and there we started praying. Soon, during our prayer, Paulette said, "Sister Thelma, the Lord says your program shall be called 'A Woman of God' because your mission is to represent God to women throughout the world. Since you have been faithful and a model of what a woman of God should be, your ministry will be a living example of a virtuous woman. Be proud to name your program, 'A Woman of God Ministries.'"

Wow! When she got through speaking, there was nothing else for me to do but accept the direction of God. Now I'm grateful to God for allowing me the privilege of being called a woman of God. I'm humbled by how God has used this name to encourage others to know him personally. And I'm not ashamed anymore.

In Ghana, I witnessed the great faith of the Christian natives, their bold love for Jesus, and how they were unashamed to proclaim him as Lord. They proclaim the name of Jesus in writing in everything they do. In the expression of his holy name they find solace and hope.

Outlandish as these commercial expressions may be, we Americans ought to be so bold. Remember the apostle Paul's words: "I am not ashamed of the gospel, because it is the power of God for the salvation of everyone who believes" (Rom. 1:16).

*If we want to be witnesses like Jesus, our only concern should be to be as alive with the love of God as Jesus was.*

HENRI NOUWEN

# *Sheep Tending*

More than thirty years ago, I had the privilege of becoming involved with a ministry that has since served thousands due to the grace of God and the vision of Dr. Robert H. Wilson Sr. As the pastor at that time of my church, St. John Missionary Baptist, Dr. Wilson founded the Office of Social Services, with the intent of supplying food, clothing, housing, medical assistance, and education to the Oak Cliff neighborhood in Dallas, Texas. When the office opened, Mrs. Edwina Cox Evans became the executive director, and I became a board member.

People with urgent needs began coming from all over the city and county because they could not qualify for assistance anywhere else. There were so many dire needs that in 1976 the Office of Social Services became a nonprofit organization called the Bethlehem Foundation (referred to as the B.F.). This was an appropriate name because *Bethlehem* means "House of Bread" in Hebrew. Over the years the Bethlehem Foundation grew to include a tutorial program, juvenile prevention and offender program, drug and alcohol treatment counseling center, rent and utility assistance, summer youth program, and AIDS and HIV assistance center.

As a board member alongside the same executive director all these years, I have seen the B.F. thrive in good times and lean times. At times it has struggled as much as the clients it serves. The church still provides some financial assistance, but most of the funds are donations from individual contributions or grants. Financially, thangs ain't been purty a lot of the time. However, in our worst times, the board has always been blown away by the commitment, dedication, creativity, faith, and stubborn love of the executive director.

Mrs. Evans and I can get into some pretty heated arguments about where the next nickel is coming from. To be honest, sometimes she gets on my last nerve. Some of the board members have even thought about closing down. But not Mrs. Evans. More than once she has tearfully, or with fire in her eyes, reminded us, "This is the Lord's program! He put me here to help people. *He* will tell us when it's time to close shop. He is ever aware of our needs, and he has promised to meet them. Don't you know that the cattle on a thousand hills are his? All he has to do is sell one cow! You board members can go your merry way if you want to, but I'm not budging until the Lord says so!"

Mrs. Evans's words challenge the eight of us to keep our focus on the mission Jesus gave Simon Peter in John 21:17, "If you love me, feed my sheep." Mrs. Evans knows that before the gospel will be openheartedly understood, believed, and received, people's bellies must be full, their bodies clothed, and their shelter provided. She lives by the saying "And they'll know we are Christians by our love." Her love for people extends to putting her personal needs on hold, taking strangers into her home, and counseling many for hours. This love of hers is above and beyond anything I have ever witnessed in my life (and I've been a part of several charitable organizations). There are few boundaries around what Mrs. Evans will do to maintain the integrity of the B.F. and, at the same time, fulfill the needs of people. As a result, thousands upon thousands of people have come to know Jesus Christ as their personal Savior because they've seen his character of love in action.

A few months ago I was sitting in the bathtub, reminiscing. I was reflecting on my fifty-nine years (fifty-five of them as a member of the same church!) and imagining that I was at the judgment seat of Christ. Imagine with me, if you will. . .

Jesus is looking in the Book of Life. Sure, my name is there. And there are a lot of notations next to it. Yes, I visited prisoners a few times. I was good about sending get-well, sympathy, and birthday cards. I occasionally visited the sick and prayed for them. There were times when I went through my closet and gave away nice clothes and shoes and even shared food from my kitchen cabinets and freezer. Oh, and don't forget the money. God made note of how much money I had given to help the poor. He remembered when I took in a young girl who was a friend of my daughter and kept her for several years through high school and college, treating her like she was my own child.

Jesus went down the list of things I had done. But it concerned me when he asked, "Why, Thelma? Why did you do all this? Was it for me, or for you? Did you do it because you love me and want to be obedient? Did you do it because you love people with the kind of tenacious, unconditional, stubborn love with which I love you every day you draw breath? Or did you do it to impress people and make a name for yourself? Thelma, have you really fed my sheep?"

As I soaked, I thought about a wonderful book I'd read a couple of years before called *This Was Your Life* by Rick Howard and Jamie Lash. The essence of the book is that we who minister must work with a sole purpose in mind: for the glory of God. I encourage you to read 1 Corinthians 3 about what it means to be "God's fellow workers" (v. 9). When we build upon the right foundation, which is Christ and his glory, then once we get to the judgment seat of Christ, when all our works are tried by the fire, they will not be burned up. Instead, we will receive stacks of gold, silver, and precious stones for our service. In short, it's only what we do for Christ that will last forever and "reap the fruit of unfailing love" (Hosea 10:12).

It is certain that what we give to others will come back to us. Isn't that what he promised: what we sow, we will also reap if we do not give up (Gal. 6:7–9)? That's God's faithful, stubborn love in action. The psalmist reflects that our faithful God will never forsake us or leave us begging for bread (Ps. 37:25). In fact, he promises that when we give, we will be given to—in "good measure, pressed down, shaken together and running over" (Luke 6:38).

The love of God is boundless, outlandish, stubborn—like Mrs. Evans's. She has spent most of her life tending God's sheep. What about you?

*Love is that condition in which the happiness of another person is essential to your own.*

ROBERT HEINLEIN

# Ooey-Gooey Bible Love

When I was a teenager, one of the Sunday school teachers in the youth department at our church enticed us to read the juiciest, most sensual love story ever written. He said it was better than any romance novel, and once we started reading it we would not want to put it down. He aroused our curiosity so much that we wanted him to be quiet so we could start reading. Once we started, we discovered he was right: we couldn't put it down.

I had forgotten just how good the story was until my friend Dee told me about her new business in California called Song of Solomon. She customizes engagement, wedding, and anniversary gift baskets using this beautiful love story as the basis for the contents. The baskets contain bath oil, dusting powder, perfume, lingerie, and all sorts of goodies to stimulate a romantic, blissful experience. I had asked her to send baskets to several brides-to-be as shower gifts. All the brides called to rave about the most unusual and perfect gift they'd received. Their response piqued my interest to revisit the spicy book of my youth.

The Song of Solomon (or Song of Songs as it is sometimes called) is a moving, dramatic love story featuring a Jewish maiden and her lover, King Solomon. This dialogue of betrothal, marriage, and sex is placed in the proper perspective—according to God's perfect plan. The beautiful, romantic, sensual, affirming love story is a tale with two meanings. One is the love and affection between the girl and the king; the other is the love and affection between Jesus and his bride—the church.

Do you remember how you felt when you became infatuated with your first love? You know, you wanted to be with him all the time, talk to him, look deep into his eyes, and hold his hand. Everything he said was either funny or right. I remember when I fell in love with my husband, George. I would sit on my front porch and pray for him to drive by just so I could see him for one second.

When Solomon's beloved recalls their courtship, she reminisces with these tender words:

Listen! My lover!
Look! Here he comes,
leaping across the mountains,
bounding over the hills.
My lover is like a gazelle or a young stag.
Look! There he stands behind our wall,
gazing through the windows,
peering through the lattice.
My lover spoke and said to me,
"Arise, my darling,
my beautiful one, and come with me.
See! The winter is past;
the rains are over and gone.
Flowers appear on the earth;
the season of singing has come,
the cooing of doves
is heard in our land.
The fig tree forms its early fruit;
the blossoming vines spread their fragrance.

Arise, come, my darling;
my beautiful one, come with me.

SONG OF SONGS 2:8–13

And when they get engaged, King Solomon says to
her:

How beautiful you are, my darling!
Oh, how beautiful!
Your eyes behind your veil are doves.
Your hair is like a flock of goats
descending from Mount Gilead.
Your teeth are like a flock of sheep just shorn,
coming up from the washing.
Each has its twin;
not one of them is alone.
Your lips are like a scarlet ribbon;
your mouth is lovely.
Your temples behind your veil
are like the halves of a pomegranate.
Your neck is like the tower of David,
built with elegance;
on it hang a thousand shields,
all of them shields of warriors.
Your two breasts are like two fawns,
like twin fawns of a gazelle
that browse among the lilies.
Until the day breaks
and the shadows flee,
I will go to the mountain of myrrh
and to the hill of incense.
All beautiful you are, my darling;
there is no flaw in you.

SONG OF SONGS 4:1–7

Now if the love between these two isn't lavish, I don't know what is! There are eight chapters in this altogether lovely book of romantic poetry. In chapter eight, the maiden emphasizes that love is as strong as death because it cannot be killed by time or disaster. "Many waters cannot quench love; rivers cannot wash it away" (Song of Songs 8:7). It cannot be bought with a price because it is freely given. It must be accepted as a gift from God and then shared within the guidelines God provides.

I encourage you to get yourself a cup of tea, curl up in your favorite chair, and read this wonderful story about the love of one girl and one king and how their love illustrates God's boundless, fearless, stubborn, lavish, outlandish, intentional love for you. God's love is sweeter than honey dripping from a honeycomb, more beautiful than the first flowers in spring, cozier than a warm blanket on a winter night, peaceful as the gentlest breeze, vast as the full moon surrounded by the endless galaxies, comfortable as a good night's rest.

And now these three remain: faith, hope and love.
But the greatest of these is love.

1 CORINTHIANS 13:13

How much more lavish can love get!
Lonely? Longing to be swept off your feet? Fall madly in love with the Lover of your soul—Jesus!

# Watch-Night Service

"Mama, we've decided that we don't want to go to a party or a church service on New Year's Eve. We don't want to be with strangers. We want to be at home with you and Daddy."

*Huh? Is this my son on the telephone?*

"We'll come over around 10:00 P.M. and play games, talk, and fellowship with each other. At 11:00, I was thinking we could start our own worship service. Little George can pray, I'll read the Scripture, Lesa and Vikki can sing, and Daddy can do whatever he wants. Then, Mama, you can bring us the message. But please limit your talk to ten minutes, okay? You know how you are when you get wound up. Just ten minutes, Mama. How does all that sound to you?"

*Ummmm ...* I actually had my own ideas for New Year's Eve that did not include being at home. Our church was planning a big to-do with a watch-night service and breakfast after midnight. And that's where George and I had thought we'd be. But as I quickly mulled over my son's suggestions, I started to get excited. Just think, our grown children wanted to close out the old year and start the new millennium at home with their *parents.* (Hmmm ... they were either really afraid of Y2K, or they really love their parents.) I knew they'd been invited to parties and other events, but they wanted to be with us. As a family. I really started liking the idea.

What's a New Year's Eve party without balloons, noise-makers, confetti, fresh flowers, and delicious food? So off I went to get everything ready for this historic night. Then I thought, *At church we would be having testimony service and communion.* So I called each of my children and told them to think about the times in their lives that were the most important turning points for them. I asked my husband to do the same.

Finally, the big day came. December 31, 1999. Beautiful gold and white balloons adorned a magnificent fresh flower centerpiece on the dining table. The tablecloth was accented with gold lamé ribbons, as were the backs of the dining chairs. Gold silverware, gold-ringed goblets, and gold and white dinner and beverage napkins surrounded the gold-trimmed china. White candles set in gold candlesticks illuminated the room. Oh yes, honey, I also wore gold and white. I had found a gold lamé sweater and a long white silk skirt in my closet. Everything was perfectly coordinated and in place.

In my office area where we would play games and have our service, I prepared another table. You guessed it—with white and gold accents. If the aroma of the food cooking on the stove didn't bait everyone, then the scent of the cinnamon spice candles throughout the house would. Music played softly in the background, offering a soothing, sweet atmosphere to the already enchanting evening.

My son's family came early—at 8:30 P.M. They knew I had cooked turnip greens, sweet potatoes, macaroni and cheese, baked chicken, roast pork loin, chitterlings, black-eyed peas, corn bread, peach cobbler, and salad. Yum, yum. Nothing was too good for my family that night— absolutely nothing. I wanted to lavish my love on them so that they would always remember the turn of the century that they'd chosen to spend with each other.

We looked at old pictures and reminisced about the past, played games, and ate. Honey, did we eat! Our worship service started around 11:00. It was so touching to hear each family member give testimony to God's blessings in their lives. Afterward, we shared communion. My son, George, had just finished praying when the clock struck midnight. Everything was perfect!

As we retired to the den to watch the fireworks on television, I noticed that my son was not in a hurry to leave. He and his wife had said earlier that they would leave right after midnight in order to visit with a few friends. But everybody sat around in the den and got so involved in watching the new millennium festivities that we all lost track of time. We oohed and aahed at the fireworks, laughed, joked, told stories, and when I finally looked at my watch, it was nearly 5:00 A.M. My whole family was still there! All the excessiveness and extravagance that I had put into making that evening special was worth it!

Isn't that what God does for us? He makes all things beautiful for us. He prepares a table before us, even in the presence of our enemies. He provides the Bread of Life to fill our hungry souls. He illuminates the dark places, and he offers us rest. He promises to withhold no good thing from us, and he gives us people to love. He loves us extravagantly, far beyond anything we can comprehend.

In my humanity, I was limited in what I could do to create the perfect festive experience for my children and grandchildren. Perhaps if I had to plan the evening over, I would do something different. But God never has to redo or undo anything for us. Every event and experience is perfectly created for our edification. God gives us the freedom each day to come into his presence and enjoy sweet fellowship with him. Often, when we don't come voluntarily, he pays us a visit, because he never wants us to think we're far from his thoughts.

> How precious to me are your thoughts, O God!
> How vast is the sum of them!
> Were I to count them, they would outnumber the grains of sand.
> When I awake, I am still with you.
>
> PSALM 139:17–18

Next time you have a moment's doubt about how much God loves you, meditate on those verses. Bask in his infinite attention and steadfast presence. Glory in his lavish love. And then give it away.

Honey, you are *LOVED* ... so far beyond your imagining!

# Let's Have a Party!

I love a celebration! And every day at my great-grand-parents' house was a celebration as I grew up under their tender care. They'd praise God for anything and everything. They held prayer meetings in our house. They would sing and pray and read the Scriptures with some of the people in our church and neighborhood. Sometimes these meetings would get so loud that I'd get embarrassed because I thought people outside could hear us. Nevertheless, I was right there in the middle with them, partying in the presence of the Lord!

In my world growing up, praise and worship were revered. You could walk into the sanctuary of our church and feel the presence of the Lord in a palpable way. As a young girl, I didn't know how to identify what that feeling was, but I felt a peacefulness come over me in church unlike in any other place. Sunday was so special to me. It was my favorite day of the week because it was a high, holy day of worship and praise for all of us.

People in our church would sing or pray or testify until they got "happy" and began shouting. That same joy still flows in some of our churches today. I remember being with author Anne Lamott when she described her church. She says that when she first started attending this primarily black church, the moans and groans of "amen" and outcries of "hallelujah" bothered her. She had not experienced emotions like that in church before. She thought of them as distractions to hearing the "real" message. But as she grew more accustomed to those sounds, she understood the genuine praise and worship they portrayed, and she grew to appreciate them. She remembers when one of the older men of the church died, and how much she missed his voice of thunderous praise — the holy sound of true worship.

Praise and worship doesn't only happen in church, of course. It can happen anywhere. As a little girl, I would sing all the time in the privacy of my great-grandparents' little back-alley apartment. I would sing old hymns and choruses like "Nearer My God to Thee," "What a Friend We Have in Jesus," and "Jesus Loves Me, This I Know." I'd sing those songs and feel something swelling up in my spirit. I didn't know what it was, but my eyes would begin to fill up and tears would run down my round cheeks. This emotion, this exuberance, this *Presence* would overpower me. It was like a celebration in my heart. It was a party!

However, as I grew older and allowed life's challenges to encumber my childlike, praiseful spirit, I would wonder, *Why do I need to spend my precious time praising the Lord when I could be doing so many other things like speaking to groups, playing with my children, romancing my husband, or exploring new adventures?* Life certainly has a way of getting in the way sometimes! But I quickly noted that as I decreased my praise time, my joy also decreased. I found out that when I made a habit of intentionally giving God the praise he deserves, I appreciated life so much better.

Take a look outside. What do you see? Do you see blue skies, rainbows, moonlit nights, twinkling stars in a vast galaxy? Do you feel the summer breeze, the fat drops of spring rain, the soft icy snowflakes on your tongue? Can you smell the fragrance of the fresh-mown grass and budding flowers? Not one twig on a tree bends, not one petal falls from a flower, without God's permission. He made all and controls all in heaven and on earth. So we praise him because of the splendor, majesty, and glory of his creation. "Let them praise the name of the LORD, for his name alone is exalted; his splendor is above the earth and the heavens" (Ps. 148:13).

We also praise God because we are recipients of his mighty acts of salvation and redemption. When Adam and Eve disobeyed their Creator, the whole human race was lost in sin. Then God came down to earth in human flesh as Jesus and claimed us back to himself. Jesus Christ died on a cruel, rugged cross to purchase our salvation through his blood. Those who have accepted him as Lord and Savior have been reclaimed as children of the Most High God! We have been saved from the ravages of sin. We are promised eternal life with God, the Creator; Jesus, his Son; and the Holy Spirit, our ever-present Comforter. Now that's a reason to praise him!

And not only have we been redeemed and saved by the blood of Jesus, but God also delivers us from everyday problems. He rescues us from situations that seem impossible. He often heals our sicknesses and diseases. He calms our anxious hearts. When we have problems, disappointments, and tough decisions to make, he reminds us through his Word that he is in control of it all. No sickness or disease, financial dilemma, loss of a loved one, addiction, distress, peril, disaster, danger, or anything else can ever separate us from his protection, guidance, and boundless love. Now that makes me shout, "Hallelujah!"

Finally, God causes us to prosper. God's gift of prosperity goes far beyond money or luxuries. His favor extends to all areas of our lives as he meets our physical, emotional, and spiritual needs. Many of our wants are provided as well because God showers us with his blessings. And I mean *all* of us. Each and every one. God doesn't love me any more than he loves you. I don't have a monopoly on God's love and grace. He has assured us all through his Word that he will keep us in perfect peace if we keep our minds on him (Isa. 26:3).

Most of the time, as soon as my feet hit the floor in the morning, I turn on praise music. I love gospel music; it gets me going! In fact, when people enter my home, they will almost always hear music playing. There's something about listening to praise music that opens up the portals of heaven on earth and reassures me that I'm surrounded by God's loving presence.

My great-grandmother used to sing, "I woke up this morning with my mind stayed on Jesus." As a morning ritual my husband sings (in the shower), "I know the Lord will make a way! Oh yes, he will." I take music on the road with me when I travel. It's an integral part of my lifestyle, and I love it.

Sometimes I even dance! Now, I'm not a good dancer, but I can dance before the Lord. Sometimes I pretend to be Miriam and dance all over my house. The gospel artist Fred Hammond recorded a song that says, "When the Spirit of the Lord comes upon my heart, I will dance like David danced." Well, sometimes I'm dressed almost like David (barely clad), and I dance before the Lord with vigor and in reverence to his holy name.

Another way I praise God is to be silent before him. "But the LORD is in his holy temple; let all the earth be silent before him" (Hab. 2:20). Sometimes it's hard just to be quiet. But Scripture says that it's in quietness and trust that we find our strength in the Lord (Isa. 30:15). So why don't you try it for a minute? Take one minute just to be silent before the Lord. Then as you reflect on your life and how God has provided for you, stand up, raise your hands in praise, open your mouth, and shout, "Praise the Lord! Thank you, Father! You've been so good to me!"

What you'll discover as you intentionally give your heart to God in praise is that he will praise you back! In fact, Scripture says that God actually sings over us when we praise him. "He will rejoice over you in great gladness. . . . Is that a joyous choir I hear? No, it is the Lord himself exulting over you in happy song" (Zeph. 3:17 TLB).

So, dear friend, whether you are surrounded by a huge crowd or resting in your bed, praise God in the morning, praise him in the noonday, praise him in the evening. Let everything that has breath praise the Lord!

God doesn't love me any more than he loves you! Together, let's praise his wonderful name. It's time to *party!*